Mission

means

Connecting

Society of African Missions

2022 – Rome

Mission means Connecting, Bulletin No. 155

© 2022 SMA publications
Cover picture by Quang Nguyen Vinh, www.pexels.com
All rights reserved
Available on Amazon sites.

ISBN: 9798819187432

Previous Bulletins

SMA publications
Società delle missioni africane
Via della Nocetta, 111, Roma 00164, Italia

www.smainternational.info
media@smainternational.org

Table of Contents

Spotlight: connecting with ...

Editorial

Mission means connecting and missionaries build bridges and become bridges!

Long distances and loads of differences create the illusion that we are isolated islands, but bridges become visible signs of the invisible connection we have always had since the time of creation. Our faith tells us that our creator is our connecting thread, and mission makes that connection visible.

A bridge belongs to both sides. It connects the two, compromises none and trusts both. In this connection we see how love is capable of leaping, trusting, and hanging in the air, vulnerable.

Jesus bridged humanity and divinity, meaning, He is fully human and fully divine. Every step we take, being inspired by this model, becomes mission. We establish the fundamental connection first, and the discussion of dogmas comes later. In this bulletin, we look at many ways we have been establishing such connections throughout our history.

We have three major sections. The first section 'Roots' is dedicated to our distant past, the second section 'Vision' to our desired future and the third section 'Spotlight' to our lived present.

Our Roots

Melchior has muscles! That is the message of the first article written by **Michael O'Shea**. Let us not be fooled by those soft eyes seen in our Founder's portrait! Brésillac had a taste for what was tough! He chose what was adventurous when he had easier alternatives. The article highlights with a lively sense of humour the braver and tougher side of Brésillac and helps us to see its role in the life of a missionary and that of a Christian.

The next article comes from **Bruno Semplicio** who navigates between the writings of our Founder, those of various modern thinkers and the encyclical *Fratelli Tutti* of Pope Francis. If everything boils down to our basic brotherhood, does today's life with all modern technologies help us to strengthen our bonds or are there illusions? While tackling this question, Bruno also highlights the key topics that dominate our society today like migration, gender equality, racism ...etc irrespective of religious, national, and economic differences. We come to understand that brotherhood among missionaries is inseparable from their mission, and communion is an essential part of the human vocation.

Learning languages is both a challenge and a joy for missionaries. People feel deeply respected and loved when they see missionaries learning their languages. Barriers break and foreigners become like family members when they speak the language of the land. Many of our SMA missionaries have not only learnt but also have contributed a lot to various languages. We are thrilled to lay hands on many dictionaries and grammar books written or compiled by our confreres. **Roberta Grossi**, the assistant archivist at the Generalate, has gone through all that we have and makes an interesting presentation with the scholarly precision of her article.

Egypt is special for the Society of African Missions since this is the African country that received the family of Jesus as migrants and asylum seekers (whatever the frontiers were then). The SMA has a long and rich mission history in Egypt. We built unique bridges there – an exemplary relationship with the Coptic Church, both Orthodox and Catholic. **Vilsan Kodavatikanti** presents the life and the contribution of Fr. Jacob Muyser SMA, an important pioneer in this area. Vilsan goes on to talk about the contribution of other SMA missionaries who followed Fr. Muyser and his own personal experience in Egypt where he worked for six years.

Our Vision

In this section, we have four articles; the first one comes from **Dominic Vincent Xavier**, a trained anthropologist serving in Benin. Dominic is a member of the SMA-OLA Commission for Inter-religious and Inter-cultural Dialogue. He discusses an area that has been part of our tradition but is hardly spoken of – the relationship with traditional leaders of the territory. His research and personal experience show him not only the prejudices towards each other of both the local leaders and the missionaries, but also the natural human expectations and even the longing of the leaders to be considered and respected by missionaries, especially in a context where the leaders are neither rich nor highly qualified in academic fields. Building bridges with traditional leaders and maintaining them are valuable for good missionary work, and they are essential for good Christian living.

In the next article, **Richard Angolio** shares his experience and reflection on brotherhood on behalf of the SMA Spirituality Commission. The article is written against the backdrop of the brutal violence in Northern Nigeria where Richard had to see the corpses of his own parishioners, killed for the sole reason that they were Christians. The dust has not fully settled down, nor have some questions. What can we preach to Christians when they know that their oppressors hear the opposite from their pulpits? Can a bridge be built depending just on the good will of one side only? Richard confronts our faith with our lived reality and vice versa.

Charles Adjoumani, who is doing his doctorate in missiology shares part of his work which is in line with our theme. How to bridge the gap between our traditional beliefs and our Christian faith so that we celebrate both the traditional identity and the Christian one, without having to choose one or the other. What are the key challenges in this area for deeper evangelisation? Following the metaphor of Pope Francis, the shepherds need to know the smell of the sheep – have a deeper knowledge of the sheep; the shepherds need to smell like the sheep – through their proximity with the sheep; Can the sheep also smell like the Shepherd? Can we smell like Jesus? Though Jesus challenged a certain Jewish practices, he was at home with His culture and with His message. Can an African own that message while still being fully African?

Francis Rozario, a member of the General Council, writes on the Original Wisdom of Inclusion. Based on the fundamental conviction that every human being is part of the ongoing projects of humanity that are bigger than any individual, Rozario discusses the dynamics of continuity, and the imperative nature of an inclusive lifestyle. A closer look at the way God treated human beings both at creation and at re-creation, reveals more clearly the logic ingrained in our nature. Jesus started His ministry by recruiting His successors! We do not prepare a handover at the end of a task, but we plan it at the beginning, and shape it at every step of the way.

Spotlight: Connecting with ...

As the title of the section indicates, the articles here focus on various ministries of our time that create connections with different sections of the society. Sometimes they are called 'special ministries', and this label evokes mixed feelings and reactions. These ministries focus on those at the margins of the society. They serve as a paradigm for the entire missionary vocation. The road to the periphery leads to the centre of our missionary identity! Even when a missionary is celebrating Mass in a packed parish church, his heart goes to those outside the windows, those the eyes cannot see.

Where did **Daniel Cardot** go after finishing his mandate as the Superior General of the SMA? He went back to the peripheries that were at the core of his missionary and Christian convictions. He worked with the *asylum-seeking migrants* in France who were extremely vulnerable as foreigners without proper documentation in an era where your existence on the planet is closely tied up with the existence of your records in various offices. Partly due to this, many people remain invisible to a big part of the society though they live at the heart of busy cities. Daniel shares his rich and challenging experience of finding meaning in the missionary vocation amid uncertainties, fears, and tears on one side and the feelings of hope, joy, and gratitude on the other.

Leprosy is being eradicated in the world today but many of those who have contracted the disease realise that they have embarked on a journey of no return! Leprosy has changed their lives and their world forever. For many, leprosarium will be the world for the rest of their lives. Jesus went out of a village to meet with a leper, and SMA missionaries have gone out from their churches to meet Jesus in lepers in many countries over the years. **Francis Athimon** who worked in the *Leprosarium of Adzope, Ivory Coast* writes in his article about his experience. While praying with people for whom leprosy is part of their collective identity, Francis feels embarrassed, disturbed, and hurt by the wording of a prayer and asks for a liturgical reform. The prayer on the offerings of the feast of the Transfiguration reads, "Cleanse us from the leprosy of sin".

Leprosy is a distant metaphor for many, but a devastating reality too close to the surface for those in a leprosarium. The use of the word leprosy in connection with sin, adds insult and guilt to the existing injury. It is a precious and powerful example that shows how our eyes open to a reality when one of us goes and utters the prayer from the other side. He felt their pain, and it pains us now. He has become a bridge connecting us with those in the leprosarium.

In the next article we discover a world where music and silence can go together. In the world of those with hearing disabilities, sound is unnecessary for communication and celebration alike. Two of our confreres are working with communities of *people with hearing disabilities* in two different countries – **Rene Dan Yao Kouamé** in Ghana and **Frank Wright** in the United States. The society is often deaf to the cries of the deaf, who feel like fish out of water in a noisy world. In many societies their cries are not heard, their needs are not met, and strangely they themselves remain invisible. This unfortunately happens even in our churches. Rene, in his article writes about the experience of starting the Deaf Mission Apostolate in 2020 which is the first of its kind in the Ghana. Frank shares his experience with a well-established deaf community. We heard the slogan "Nothing about us, without us" during the Amazonian Synod, Frank echoes the same idea from the deaf communities and informs us that the coordinator for Deaf Ministry in Washington DC is herself deaf. This jumps out as an important point for all types of ministries. Everybody needs love and support, but nobody wants to be patronised and belittled even in the name of pastoral care. This is an extension of the intimate missionary conviction of our Founder, "Unhappy the country where the voice of a missionary is never heard. But still unhappy is the country that has only missionaries to look at."[1]

Building bridges applies also to parish ministry. We have two confreres who share their experiences of reaching out and living real brotherhood in their missions - **Mariel Sumallo** in *Tanzania*, and **Yakubu Sabo Salisu** in *Angola*.

Mariel sums up saying "At the end of the day, it's the quality of an encounter that will leave a mark upon the hearts of the

---

[1] MELCHIOR DE MARION BRESILLAC, Art 5, *Mission and Foundation Documents*, Paris 1985, 80.

people, and hopefully, bring them closer to God." The brotherhood we live in our ministry matters more than any project we do. Yakubu Sabo shows how challenging it is to rebuild community, brotherhood, and family spirit in a country that was torn by wars and conflicts. It takes longer to build a community than a cathedral!

Tanga house in Tanzania is one of the newest bridges we have built! **Janusz Machota** and the missionary team in Tanga house help us to discover another world of the vulnerable – *people with albinism*. The lack of melanin in the body hurts people with albinism a lot and the lack of understanding and acceptance hurts them even more. The article presents a clear picture of the challenges faced by our brothers and sisters born with this condition and explains how the Tanga house was created as a family house from where the members can relate to the world with confidence and dignity. It is very interesting to read here about the reservations that had to be overcome when building bridges with some sponsors who do not share our values and at the same time "Nobody has the monopoly on doing good"!

I express my sincere gratitude and appreciation to all those who have contributed to this bulletin with enthusiasm and generosity. I thank Andrea Mandonico, Brice Afferi, Dolores Mc Crystal, Michel Bonemaison, Pierre Paul Dossekpli, Sylvere Atta, and Wacek Dominic for their generous help in translating and proofreading.

This is an invaluable collection of our convictions, our missionary convictions. What emerges from here is a missionary paradigm that can be summed up in three words: Going – Connecting – Growing.

Missionaries move to cutting edges without cutting ties with their communities of origin. In fact, they are sent by their Churches of origin as representatives.

This is not only to see foreigners but to feel and live as life is felt and lived by our family members at the peripheries. This is connecting with some members of the human family as representatives of some other members of the same family. What happens next? Eyes open on all sides. People start seeing with their hearts, as Pope Francis says in *Fratelli Tutti*.[2]

Growth becomes inevitable. Growth involves changes. As prejudices and perspectives change, it will not be too long before we see changes all over, from the liturgy of the Church to the legislation in the world. This is evolution, in more familiar words, the growth of the Kingdom.

Connecting enriches more than giving, sharing life transforms more than leading, growing together becomes collective and continual conversion. Real growth of humanity comes from real connections.

Go without leaving!
Connect without condescending!!
Grow, with the whole of humanity, grow!!!

S. I. Francis Rozario SMA

---

[2] *"Its point of departure must be God's way of seeing things." God does not see with his eyes, God sees with his heart."* POPE FRANCIS, Encyclical letter *Fratelli Tutti* (3 Oct 2020). n. 281.

Our Roots

Muscles and Melchior

Michael O'Shea SMA

Since the cause for canonisation of our Founder was first mooted some forty years ago, the Society has focussed on his holiness. Now that the Vatican has endorsed his 'heroic virtues' (May 2020) no doubt more ink will be spilled on his virtues. Here, I'd like to focus on his *natural* virtues: ones like **strength, courage, and stamina.**

Melchior de Marion Brésillac, first born of his family grew up to be a robust country boy of pleasant mien and personality. Familiar with the outdoor life, he loved horse riding, walking and climbing the hills of home – "the lovely landscape of Languedoc where I spent the best years of my life".[1] His homeland was an inland agricultural and vine growing area and his life span was post Revolution edging into the beginning of the industrial age. Likely he included himself in the quotation, "We the rough and violent Gauls";[2] he certainly did not consider himself "a nervous type".[3] His proud father remarking on his son's physical strength warned him not to let it get him into danger. He was a daring and free young man in his home environment, but what was he like in unfamiliar locations?

His first experience of a very different environment was the sea, encountered in his voyage to India. It did not scare him one bit despite a bad storm which nearly wrecked the ship as soon as it left the port of Paimboeuf in northern France. Twelve years later, returning from India

---

[1] MELCHIOR DE MARION BRÉSILLAC, *Souvenirs*, Rome 1988, 729.
[2] *Ibid.*, 318.
[3] *Ibid.*, 809.

an even worse storm endangered his ship in the Mediterranean. Despite an initial bout of sea sickness, he actually revelled in the fury of the sea and the wind. Next morning, with the storm becoming ever more dangerous he struggled back on deck "in order to really enjoy the magnificent horrors of the present situation".[4] The Captain concerned for his safety invited him into his cabin where he could watch 'the spectacular show' with more safety. The storm continued unabated for a few days, but Brésillac remaining faithful to his ordinary routine, said his breviary 'in its entirety', and had his breakfast as usual when no others, not even some of the ship's officers, could stomach anything.[5]

As a missionary frequently on the move in torrid India he rode a jaded old horse which he'd bought for the meagre sum of 21 rupees - all he could afford at the time. In honour of the price tag he wittily named the horse 'Vingt et un' (Twenty One). On one occasion when he fell off, rather than blame the horse, he wittily said it was the one day he'd forgotten to say the Itinerary Prayer.[6]

In travelling in India, he also risked plenty of dangers on rivers and lakes, dangers at which most ordinary travellers would baulk. Crossing the River Cavery in a tiny parrisal (a bamboo basket covered with buffalo hides) when the mighty river was in flood did cost him a thought but did not deter him. In fact, he described the experience as "a wonderful adventure which made [him] forget all his travel-weariness".[7]

As a bishop going to officiate at the episcopal ordination of Mgr. Canoz sj in faraway Trichinopoly, being again short of funds he opted to go with Fr. Pacreau from Codivelly mission near the Bhavani river by parrisal, though previously he had cautioned the same Pacreau not to use this method of travel as it was too dangerous. It was a long downstream voyage from Codivelly on the Bhavani river to its confluence with the Cavery and then down the Cavery to Trichy, a five-or-six day hazardous journey especially as both rivers were in flood. For Brésillac to get to Codivelly from his base at Karumattampatty he had first an eight-or-nine hour journey to do 'on a very poor horse'.[8]

---

[4] Ibid.,1324.

[5] Ibid.,1325.

[6] BRUNO SEMPLICIO, De Marion Brésillac (1813 – 1859). Bishop and Founder of the Society of African Missions, Rome 2005, 142.

[7] MELCHIOR DE MARION BRÉSILLAC, Souvenirs, 271.

[8] Ibid., 805.

For their cost saving voyage Pacreau had two large parrisals built (for the princely price of 5 rupees each!) but he warned the bishop to bring a chair and a parasol with him as otherwise the trip would prove very uncomfortable there being no seating or shelter aboard.[9] The voyage was hair-raising but the bishop exulted in it and observed everything from the sharp rocks that lay treacherously in their path, to the skill of the paddlers and pole men in avoiding them. Nor did he fail to notice and comment on the myriads of riverine birds, and the wonderful fauna and flora of the banks.

For the return journey from Trichy to Karumattampatty, as going upstream by river against the current was not possible, he bought a battered old cab and an elderly horse, (altogether 150 Rupees) when he got home the cab would serve him commuting between Karumattampatty and Coimbatore which he was soon to make his headquarters. His attitude to travel was, "To a missionary what is a bit of rough travelling now and then?"[10] The overland journey back to Karumattampatty was a safe but monotonous six-day drive with none of the excitement of the downriver adventure.[11]

Some of his land journeys were even more fraught with danger than those on water on account of robbers and dangerous wild animals. Trekking through one of the wildest parts of South India much frequented by thieves, Brésillac remained calm though his attendants were far from it. He told them not to worry as he would protect them with a musket which he brandished as he rode along. However, it was only bluff - he'd no powder or shot.[12]

En route to one of the most remote outstations, he passed through 'real tiger country'. But nonchalantly joked, "I can't boast that I saw any (tigers) but if I didn't see 'em, I certainly smelt 'em".[13]

Travelling with un-named 'Fr A' to Salem in atrocious heat, both men plunged into an inviting wayside lake to cool off and the obliging midday sun gave both of them severe sunstroke. Further on the journey the two ventured into another lake but, cleverly, this time *after* sundown. However here they were attacked by blood-sucking leeches which infested the muddy-bottomed lake.[14]

---

[9] *Ibid.,* 803.
[10] *Ibid.,* 1343.
[11] *Ibid.,* 830.
[12] *Ibid.,* 214.
[13] *Ibid.,* 278.
[14] *Ibid.,* 701.

Brésillac's endurance and determination were phenomenal. For instance, on return from a visit to Colombo, Ceylon, despite suffering from fever and a violent headache, he set out for faraway Karaikal on horseback to attend an official function. Eventually pain and weakness forced him to stop and send for help to a Jesuit mission. They sent a comfortable carriage for him but on arrival at their mission he collapsed. After only a day's rest, and still very ill, he continued his journey and made it to Karaikal *on time*. On this occasion his pain was so severe he thought he was going to die. [15]

When travelling, he wanted to see everything of note, and he used his physical strength and stamina to see that he did. On his return from India he spent two days in Cairo. All too short to see much but he didn't spare himself. In one morning after gaining permission from the General in charge he visited the famous new mosque of Mohammed Ali. There he was lost in admiration and ranked it even higher in splendour than Paris's *Notre-Dame*. Among other things it had the most beautiful sanctuary he'd ever seen; he reckoned it would be one of the finest buildings in the world if the great genius, Ali, had been able to put the finishing touches to it, but he died too soon. Giving a few piastres to the caretakers, Melchior was allowed to climb to the very top of the minaret all of 400 ft above the floor. There he enjoyed an exhilarating view of all Cairo, the Nile, the deserts and the Pyramids. [16]

Despite being tired by the minaret climb, on leaving the mosque he hurried on to Joseph's Well which goes down about the same distance that the minaret goes up. After climbing down and back up, his knees were beginning to groan in agony so he hired a mule to take him back to his Franciscan convent accommodation for a meagre lunch. Afterwards, without resting he rushed off to see the Pyramids, two hours away. There, he climbed to the top of the highest one!! And after regaining ground level he descended into the pyramid's tomb. By the time he got back to the Convent he was so stiff that he had to be lifted bodily off the mule, his leg muscles had totally seized up. "Never in my life was I so thoroughly tired-out", he admitted, but he'd achieved his aims. [17]

Of the new jurisdictions, Brésillac's vicariate, Coimbatore was the most destitute lacking in finance, personnel and infrastructure. He lived frugally himself and was always on the look-out for cheap modes of

---

[15] *Ibid.,* 1144.
[16] *Ibid.,* 1309.
[17] *Ibid.,* 1312.

transport. [18] He normally travelled by bullock cart or on horseback like a simple missionary and shunned the expensive palanquin (a covered hammock, carried on the shoulders of two or four men) favoured by Government officials and some high-ranking clergy. Normally he only used such when seriously ill. [19]

On trek he slept in the public 'savady', a rough shelter in which one slept on a mat on the floor. However, in one place he actually had a bed which, though it probably contributed to a better night's sleep, it caused a near-serious accident in the morning. Waking promptly at cock crow he stepped out as if he was on a mat and fell heavily on the floor. On recovering he laughed at himself and thanked the Lord for his low stature saying if he had been an inch taller he would have cracked his head against the sharp corner of a metal trunk by the bed. As it was his luxuriant beard cushioned the blow on the hard ground. (He took it on the chin!) Jokes aside, the injury ached all day but, resisting a strong urge to rest, he continued riding to fulfil his planned itinerary. [20]

One evening around Christmas time when he failed to reach any accommodation, he passed the night in an appallingly dirty dung mired cow shed, but though grumbling at first, eventually he came to beg God's pardon when he remembered that it was in such a place that Christ was born. [21]

His father's warning about strength and risk-taking proved apt on many an occasion, not least in the following incident when even he himself felt that he'd pushed his luck too far. Returning from Karumattampatty to Coimbatore – a relatively short four-hour journey in his old cab he was surprised by a sudden violent storm. The road was blocked by a flash flood and many travellers were on the edge of the flood waiting for the waters to recede. Night had fallen. "[I] being less prudent" said Brésillac, attempted to go through the flood. Leading his horse and cab through the fast-flowing water, which came to his knees and at times to his waist he made it and went on to the next savady. This one was also crammed with cart drivers again waiting for the waters of another flooded river to go down. It was now pitch dark but he was only 3 miles from home, and if he could cross this flood the rest of the journey would be easy. [22]

---

[18] *Ibid.,* 826.

[19] *Ibid.,* 1144.

[20] *Ibid.,* 303.

[21] *Ibid.,* 367.

[22] *Ibid.,* 864.

With much pleading and many rupees, he persuaded one man to go ahead of him with a long pole to test the depth of the water. If it wasn't so dark, he would have been able to see better the width and fury of the flood and probably would not have tried to cross. Again, his luck held but his final comment was "I came very close to a watery end".[23] Indeed, at times we have to ask was his action prudent courage or mad rashness.

Some people would include enjoying 'a drink with the boys' as part of the manly ethos. On Brésillac's first trip to Salem, he shared *part* of the journey with friends Frs Triboulot and Roger but he shared with them *all* of two bottles of Bordeaux *and* a flagon of Chateau-Lafitte. After a few more years' experience he declared that one of the greatest privations of a missionary in India was the absence of wine![24]

---

[23] *Ibid.*, 864.
[24] *Ibid.*, 206.

"Fratelli Tutti" and our Fraternity

Bruno Semplicio SMA

We are all familiar with *"Fratelli Tutti"*, the encyclical letter of Pope Francis on fraternity and social friendship, published on 3 October 2020 in Assisi. In the various dioceses there have been several initiatives to publicise and discuss it. It is a document written with a view to developing a universal brotherhood in which each individual feels accepted, recognised, loved, and valued and able to live with dignity and respect. For us Christians, this is achieved above all through the love that each person is commanded to have for his or her brothers and sisters: God "created all human beings equal in rights, duties and dignity, and called them to live together as brothers and sisters".[1]

The Lord has entrusted us with the mission that sends us out into the world towards all men and women so that they may become children of God and therefore brothers. In order to do this, we need first of all to be thoroughly familiar with the recipients of our action and witness, the society in which they live, and their specific circumstances. In order to build a bridge, we need to be aware of condition of the terrain we are encountering and the state of the bank where we hope to start constructing our bridge. We also need to show by our example what it means to live and act as brothers.

---

[1] POPE FRANCIS AND AHMAD AL-TAYYEB, THE GRAND IMAM OF AL-AZHAR, "A Document on Human Fraternity for World Peace and Living Together" (Abu Dhabi, 4 February 2019).

A look at our world

The situation

The history of our world, ancient and modern, presents us with a situation where brotherhood is far from being achieved. In the first chapter of his encyclical, the Pope says that the world we are presented with is often a closed one. We see dreams which break into pieces, we do not see a project which benefits everyone, due to obstacles such as global marginalisation, human rights not universally respected, and myriad other conflicts and fears. We note the advance of globalisation and progress but without a common goal, pandemics and other shocking events, a lack of human dignity for migrants at the national borders, the false illusion of communication (blatant aggression, information without wisdom), submissiveness and self-deprecation. However, despite all its threats, we see some hopeful ways forward. In this presentation, the Pope states that he does not "pretend to make an exhaustive analysis or to take into consideration all the aspects of the reality in which we live." "I propose," he says, "only that we focus our attention on certain tendencies in the world today that impede the promotion of universal brotherhood" (FT 9).

The challenges before us

As missionaries we must focus especially on the most abandoned. To do this we need to know the challenges of our particular age, taking into account the very rapid changes that affect our society, especially in the West. Their consequences affect relationships between people, families and social groups. A serious reflection on brotherhood must take this into account. Jesus is the Word who became fully incarnate in the lived reality experienced by the men and women of his own and the surrounding countries, in their situations and needs, in their illnesses and their poverty of all kinds.

Today, we are called on to understand the rapid transformations and also the contradictions that the world of today - the target of our missionary action - is experiencing. In order to do this, we need to know some of the clues that come from the analyses made by international and world institutions that know how to study the present and prepare for the immediate future. The world is going through changes that are visible on the geopolitical, economic and social levels. Important transformations are taking place that affect people's lives. Trends are emerging which, in a short space of time, are changing people's behaviour in relation to their social, religious and family conditions and traditions. It is important to be aware of them and to make them more widely known so that those in power can control them and eliminate the negative elements. Missionary institutions should be in a position to speak out as a prophetic voice for all the abandoned of the earth.

According to Maurice Molinari, journalist and writer, in a recent publication on the subject, the most important challenges for our time are: 1. Conflicts: old and new wars, how and why we fight. 2. Sovereignty and populism: challenges to the rule of law. 3. Migration: people on the move and migration flows. 4. Imbalances: rich and poor, a growing divide. 5. The emerging climate: the health of the planet. 6. Gender equality: women and inclusion. 7. Racism: discrimination and intolerance. 8. Epidemics: global health issues. Each of these points is presented by the author with data, statistics and reports resulting from research carried out by international organisations. [2]

These challenges affect, sometimes very negatively, the lives of populations. They make relationships difficult, cause conflicts at all levels and damage the ties that exist between people of the same family, ethnicity and social class. Despite this, examples of great solidarity and fraternity are developing everywhere, giving light and hope in critical and particularly desperate situations.

The threats and dangers of a "liquid" society

According to the famous sociologist Zygmunt Bauman, we live in a perpetual and breathless present where everything is entrusted to the experience of the moment and where the loss of the sense of time is accompanied by the loss of the criteria that serve to distinguish the essential from the superfluous, what lasts and what is ephemeral. Today, he says, we live on the run, with all the consequences that this entails, for example, in social relations. [3]

The tyranny of the moment is the most obvious characteristic of contemporary society (Thomas Eriksen). Many connections and also many disconnections accompany our days. According to Helen Haste, a psychologist at the University of Bath, a third of young boys see nothing

---

[2] M. MOLINARI, *Atlante del mondo che cambia, Le mappe che spiegano le sfide del nostro tempo*, Milano 2020, 206 in: B. SEMPLICIO, *Be Holy*, Genova 2021, 214-216.

[3] Z. BAUMAN, *Vite di corsa, Come salvarsi dalla tirannia dell'effimero*, Bologna 2008, 102.

wrong with breaking off a personal relationship with a simple text message.

The culture of liquid modernity, again according to Bauman, where fragmentation dominates, is becoming the culture of disengagement, of discontinuity, of forgetting. There is therefore a need for continual, but open-ended training.

There are many indications that we are moving towards a society in which it is almost impossible to predict anything more than a sentence reduced to small pieces. It is paradoxical: "In the age of easy and instantaneous connection, characterised by the guarantee that one can be constantly in touch, the communication between the experience of the moment and what precedes or follows it, must be permanently interrupted".[4] This leads to the formation of a kind of society where people live only in the present and do not consider the past and the consequences of their actions for the future. Such an approach "translates into a lack of connection with others. The culture of the present promotes speed and efficiency and suppresses patience and perseverance" (E. Tarkowska).[5]

The challenges of digital technology

On this point, I am inspired by the reflections of Father Antonio Spadaro S.J., director of the magazine "La Civiltà Cattolica", who, in a publication, presents some considerations on faith that is "social".[6] He is a specialist in this field. Previously, he published "Cybertheology or Imagining Christianity in the era of the internet".[7] In the Preface of this book he states:

"Search engines, smartphones, applications, social networks: recent digital technologies have entered our daily lives in force. But not only as external tools, to be used to simplify communication and the relationship with the world: rather, they conceive a new anthropological space that changes our way of thinking, of knowing reality and of maintaining human relationships".

The same author emphasises that the network is a medium that "allows for experimentation with new forms of contact, relationship and

---

[4] *Ibid.*, 33-34.

[5] *Ibid.*, 35.

[6] A. SPADARO, *Quando la fede si fa social*, Bologna 2015, 62.

[7] A. SPADARO, *Cyberteologia Pensare il cristianesimo al tempo della rete*, Milano 2012.

self-expression. The places and activities where this is done are called 'social' precisely because their substance lies in the communication between the people who use them".[8]

The network must not only be a place of connection: it must become a place of communion, and the Christian must commit himself to achieving this objective. "The network does not aim to eliminate differences but to connect them, to open up dialogue, to make people feel more united".

At the end of his text, Fr. Spadaro summarises what he has written in six challenges that require a change of perspective from us:

- from pastoral focus on giving answers to focus on asking questions

- from pastoral focus on content to focus on people.

- From pastoral focus on teaching to focus on witness.

- From pastoral focus on propaganda to focus on proximity.

- From pastoral focus of ideas to focus on narration.

- Pastoral focus on interiority and interactivity.[9]

Achieving these changes has consequences for the quality of the relationships we have with others, individuals, families, groups, movements, whom we meet in our missionary and pastoral endeavours.

A witness for today's world: our fraternity

The experience of the first Christians

I regard with admiration the rapid and consistent missionary success that the first Christians, who were very few in numbers, achieved in the first two centuries in the regions subject to the Roman Empire. The challenge before them was enormous: a pagan society and world, a civil authority that persecuted them, a popular culture often based on the tyranny of the most powerful. But the proclamation of the dead and risen Jesus Christ, the faith in Him and the witness of the first communities were the message that attracted the hearts and minds of the people.

Among the Christians, from the earliest times (see Acts 2: 42-48), the faithful gathered for the hearing of the Word and the breaking of the Bread, which was followed by the service of the poor, the widows, the sick, the prisoners, the strangers, all helped by the collection of money

---

[8] A. SPADARO, *Quando*, 14-15.

[9] *Ibid.*, 60.

and goods. The communal life and the sharing of goods, especially in the most critical moments, was also a sign that aroused the admiration of the pagans. All this was done in the faith and light of the dead and risen Christ. The Letter to Diognetus is a precious testimony to the way Christians lived in the world.

Moreover, the testimony of the martyrs, who belonged to every category of people, was, according to Tertullian, the seed that gave birth to new Christians. The divisions and, at times, conflicts between Christians, caused by the first heresies and the infidelities of some, did not prevent the spread and acceptance of the Gospel.

Throughout the centuries, the history of Christian mission presents us with many difficult situations, crises, changes considered dangerous, times when even the leadership of the Church was inflicted by divisions, conflicts, and scandals. But in various ways, sometimes through the action of new prophets urged on by the Holy Spirit, the storms gave way to new horizons opening up a path for the advancement of the Gospel.

If, as they say, 21st century man is a networking man, always connected and always communicating, it should not be difficult to transform communication into communion between the sons of the same father and therefore between brothers.

Our fraternal life between the current reality and our desired future

We believe that only in Jesus Christ can everything be unified and transformed: see Eph 1, 4-12. It is in Christ and through Him that we are brothers, and it is in Him that all brotherhood is realised. We must not be afraid to proclaim him in a time when, even in the Church, his name does not resonate as it should.

Our vocation calls us to reach out to the men and women of today's world, by giving prophetic witness to them.

As I said before, today's world, especially in the West, creates obvious difficulties in interpersonal relationships and in the formation of groups trying to develop an authentic life in common. But our present age also offers us new possibilities that we need to identify and make use of in the pursuit of our mission.

Our authentic fraternal life is a fundamental condition for the success of our mission. A quick glance at our history shows that our missionary endeavours have always been accompanied by exhortations and advice on how to enhance our community life.

In our present Constitutions, we speak of the "missionary family" envisaged by our Founder (art. 23.1). It says that "... in a spirit of co-responsibility we are aware of the call that has brought us together in one family" (art. 23.2).

It is also stated that "forming apostolic communities, we have come together to share our faith and love. By this life in community we help each other to live and proclaim the Gospel in the manner of Christ and of the disciples whom he gathered to be with him" (Art. 24).

At the time of the Founder

In the time of Bishop de Brésillac, there was already a need for a fraternal life in missionary communities, even if it was expressed in terms different from ours today. In fact, we find in our Founder the desire for and commitment to unity among the missionaries, to well-prepared meetings, and to community life. In fact he suffered greatly because of the individualism of his collaborators.

Some teachings:

"Let us be very careful not to demand too much perfection. Charity can be very imprudent in this respect and produce more harm than excessive kindness or condescension" (no. 35). [10]

"I fear more harm than I hope for good from this meeting of all the missionaries. The particular spirit, the spirit of independence and a little more than that, is what is losing us. [11]

In the first edition of the Fundamental Articles for the SMA, (1856):

"Wherever several associates are together, they shall observe the common life" (Art. VIII). [12]

"The nerve of the society is concord in perfect charity" (Art. XII). This last point is taken up again in the second edition of the Fundamental Articles (1858) where the following is added:

"The aspirants, even if they have all the other qualifications, he shall not be incorporated into the association if he is seen to have too much of a spirit of independence in him or a marked reluctance to adapt to characters different to his own". [13]

---

[10] MARION BRÉSILLAC, *Documents de mission et de fondation*, Paris 1985, 90.

[11] MARION BRÉSILLAC, "To Tesson, 8 January 1849, no. 0378" in *Lettres*, Genova 2005, 677.

[12] MARION BRÉSILLAC, *Documents de mission*, 171.

[13] *Ibid.*, 222.

In a letter from our Founder to Father Planque, on the subject of the first SMA seminary, he states: "...I admit that it is absolutely necessary to aim at a spirit of greater acceptance and simplicity in the house".[14]

Constitutions and Directory

Throughout the ages, the constitutions and directories do not speak explicitly about fraternal life. They give useful indications so that each member can promote it:

"The Constitutions are the principle of good order in the Society. When properly observed, they keep each one in his own sphere, giving him the means to contribute effectively to the common work. From this order flows peace in the Society".[15]

In the Directory for the members of the SMA, published in 1957, we find an interesting text on the relationship between missionaries:

"The missionaries shall show deference and respect for each other, and, like members of the one family, live in perfect unity and real brotherly love. Each one shall try to ensure that he is in no way a burden to his confreres, and shall be prepared to bear with their physical and spiritual shortcomings without complaining or showing that they hurt. Confreres shall render each other every possible help and service, including even that of fraternal correction. Both in word and in deed, they shall be very careful to avoid anything that might offend, sadden or humiliate another, or that might give rise to discord or suspicion among their brothers and weaken the unity that should exist between them."[16]

Fraternal life for a better evangelisation

After the Second Vatican Council, in the text of the 1968 General Assembly, we find this statement:

"The members of the SMA ... are aware of the call which has brought them together in one body (Col 3: 15) and form one family which its Founder has placed under the special protection of the Holy Family. 'Persevering in fraternal charity' (Heb 13: 1), 'bearing one another's burdens according to the law of Christ' (Col 6: 2), 'eager to give hospitality' (Rom. 12: 13), they remain 'steadfast in the faith' (1 Pt. 5: 9), 'diligent in prayer, joyful in hope' (Rom. 12: 12), always 'ready to

---

[14] MARION BRÉSILLAC, "To Planque, 29 June 1857, no. 0767" in *Lettres*, Genova 2005, 1291.

[15] SOCIÉTÉ DES MISSIONS AFRICAINES DE LYON, Directoire no. 11 in *Constitutions et Directoire*, Lyons 1932, 64.

[16] SOCIÉTÉ DES MISSIONS AFRICAINES DE LYON, no. 152 in *Directory*, Cork 1957, 52.

surrender their own lives along with the Gospel of Christ' (1 Thess. 2: 8)." [17]

On the lifestyle of the members of the SMA it is stated:

B. 41: "Members of the same Society, aware of the common goal that unites them, the confreres will put charity into practice by showing courtesy and consideration to one another, consulting one another in dialogue; they will develop among themselves a true spirit of teamwork and mutual help". [18]

Similarly, in the document of the 1978 General Assembly entitled "Evangelisation and Renewal", in the chapter on spiritual renewal, number 57: "If Christ calls us, it is to invite us to live together in the Love he shares with his Father in the unity of the Holy Spirit. But it is also to send us out together and make the Gospel visible, before preaching it in words. Each community of brothers and disciples of Jesus Christ is thus the first relay of the Church, the sacrament of Salvation and Liberation. Our community life is first of all a requirement for a better evangelisation" (*Evangelii Nuntiandi* 21).

No. 59 adds that "this effort for a more authentic and true community life must also extend to the Christian communities of which we are the animators. With them we are one, and we must constantly challenge them so that together we can give an attractive witness to non-Christians who are looking for something or someone they can guess but cannot name" (E.N. 21). [19]

A family lifestyle

From 1983 onwards, the method for the work of the G.A. has changed and our subject is recalled from time to time with other terms and by taking place in the chapter "Spirituality and Lifestyle".

Thus, it is said that "(there) remains, however, the difficulty of sharing one's faith with others and of listening to them in depth" (G.A. 1995, p. 44).

The 2001 General Assembly speaks of community life, notes progress and affirms the need to "promote international apostolic life communities, centred on the mission" (p. 37).

In 2007 the G.A. vision envisages that "we act in a family spirit, open and attentive to one another, nourished by community life and the SMA team spirit" (p. 61).

---

[17] SOCIETY OF AFRICAN MISSIONS, *General Assembly 1968*, Rome 1968, 16.

[18] *Ibid.*, 30.

[19] *Ibid.*

In the 2013 G.A. in the challenges regarding spirituality and lifestyle it is stated:

"While we strive to live a true community life, our efforts are hindered by a lack of understanding of community life, a lack of sharing and solidarity, individualism and the promotion of personal projects" (p. 37).

Our last G.A. 2019 argues that "the SMA is seen as a family whose members are bound by their desire to live mission in community".

"Fratelli tutti" in the SMA

To have any influence, then, on the men and women of the 21st century we need to offer them a genuine example of fraternal life.

Following the encyclical of Pope Francis, we too need to free ourselves from certain shadows (chapter one) that obstruct our path. They are inevitable because we are all sinners. Brotherly correction according to the Gospel is often unknown and a true revision of life is rather rare. We too can fall victim to the "illusion of communication" (FT, 42-50).

However, especially in times of difficulty, exceptional gestures of solidarity, fraternity and friendship are evident in the life of our communities creating a welcoming family atmosphere that extends also to those who meet us. Some testimonies from confreres:

"The SMA is my family. We live a fraternal and simple life that I like a lot. I know that if I am having a hard time, I will have someone beside me on whom I can count".

"The SMA is first of all a family, a missionary family that has allowed me to have rich and valuable missionary experiences".

"It is the family spirit that makes me feel at home with SMA confreres everywhere. What I also like is our simple lifestyle, very close to the people".

"The simplicity in the lifestyle, the fraternity that is not cheesy but solid and frank... the fraternal mutual aid...".

"Simplicity - we don't have big heads - a certain frankness in relationships - respect for each person's journey". [20]

---

[20] SOCIETY OF AFRICAN MISSIONS, *Passionnés pour la Mission aujourd'hui*, Rome 2005, 118-121. This publication gathers the confreres' answers to a questionnaire proposed by the Spirituality Commission following a decision of the 2001 General Assembly.

The second chapter of *Fratelli Tutti*, "A stranger on the way", with the icon of the Good Samaritan, offers us useful considerations for a community life where the wounded especially can be welcomed and cared for.

The universal love that promotes people (Chapter three), propels us towards those who are far away, but must not make us forget those who are close to us.

Our hearts are genuinely open to the whole world (Chapter four) if we can experience at home the gift of living among disciples of Jesus who are of one heart and one soul (cf. Acts 4: 32). It is interesting what the Pope says about 'the effort to recognise the right of the other to be himself and to be different' (FT 218), about the need to rediscover benevolence (FT, 222-224), about the value and meaning of forgiveness (FT 236-245), and about the capacity to deal with memory (FT 246-254).

The last chapter of FT states that religions are at the service of brotherhood in the world and "we, believers believe that without an openness to the Father of all, there will be no solid and stable reasons for the call to fraternity". We are convinced that "only with this awareness of being children who are not orphans can we live in peace with others" (FT 272).

As believers and as disciples of Jesus, our fraternal life is therefore a fundamental requirement for responding to His call to make of today's humanity one family, that of the children of God. But without the Lord we can do nothing (Jn 15: 5). For this reason, Pope Francis ends the encyclical by praying: "Grant that we Christians may live the Gospel and discover Christ in every human being, to see Him crucified in the anguish of the abandoned and forgotten of this world and resurrected in every brother who rises up".

Connecting through local languages

Roberta Grossi

What is left of the original work when it is translated into several languages? This question was asked by a famous Italian poet Eugenio Montale (1896-1981) in the late 1970s. From this idea began a project to translate his poem "*Nuove Stanze*". The task was that each translator, except the first, would work not on the original but from a translation and that he would not know the identity of the author. In this way, an activity was set in motion which transposed the poem from Arabic into French, from that into Polish, and so on, until it returned to Italian as its last destination. The result of this interesting experiment is published in a booklet with the revealing title "*Poesia Travestita*"[1] (Disguised Poetry), where the original version of "*Nuove Stanze*" can be compared with the final version.

The anecdotes about the complexity of the translation work are endless. They share a basic idea about the difficulties of this work and the inevitable element of "betrayal" towards the original language. Translation, in fact, despite its irreplaceable practical function, will always contain a certain inadequacy since it passes through distant lexical worlds. Conscious of the fact that the meaning of the original word is almost never completely given, Walter Benjamin acknowledged

---

[1] E. MONTALE, M. CORTI (ED), M.A TERZOLI (ED)., *Poesia travestita*, 1999.

that the "undisciplined freedom of bad translators"[2] is sometimes more at work in this job.

The work of translation becomes more complex if it is from specific oral cultures, for example, of African populations. This is why, it seems to me that the reflections proposed by Michel de Certeau are very explanatory:

In order to speak, oral language waits for a writing to go through it and know what it says [...]. I wonder about the meaning of this word established in place of the other and intended to be heard in a diverse way (differently) from the way it speaks.[3]

The translation as "a return to the West and to writing, a return to the Christian text"[4] of European languages, contains a certain removal of: sounds, pronunciation, music of words and songs. What remains is a de-somatised language, as it happens with any writing that in transit from orality loses something related to the disappearance of the "soma" and its semantic richness.[5]

Having clarified the pitfalls still present in this kind of operation, it is interesting here to think about the concrete and productive aspects of translations as they become a "bridge" to get to the other shore, the "unknown". And, in fact, in the Italian language, the term "bridge" refers to the root "path": to go, in the sense of overcoming barriers.[6] This consideration is particularly appropriate if one is to analyse the translation work that many SMA fathers did as early as the end of the 19th century.

The SMA library in Rome has a very large collection, about 500 titles of texts translated from French and English into various African languages and dialects: sacred writings, prayers, dictionaries, grammars, exercises, rites, songs, and traditional stories. These are very often manuscripts and typed documents, but there are also many printed books. Among these, the oldest date back to the late nineteenth century, for example the proverbs in the Nago-French language (1883): "Les noirs peints par eux-mêmes" by Fr. Pierre Bertrand Bouche (1835-1903); "Katechismu e no klon dô, Dan-hô-mê" (1898) by Fr. François

---

[2] W. BENJAMIN, Il compito del traduttore, in Aut-Aut, 334/2007, 14, 16.

[3] M. DE CERTEAU, La scrittura della storia, S. FACIONI (ED), Milano 2006, 216, 223. On these pages Certeau analyses Histoire d'un voyage fait en la terre du Brésil (1578) by Jean de Léry.

[4] M. DE CERTEAU, La scrittura della storia, 233.

[5] R. BARTHES, La grana della voce. Interviste 1962-1980, Torino 1981, 243-244.

[6] https://www.etimo.it/?term=ponte.

Steinmetz (1868-1952). Among the manuscripts, I particularly emphasize the three-volume work of Fr. Joseph Corbeau (1882-1962) "*Essai de grammaire en langue Esa*" (1917) in French and English. This work is remarkable from the point of view of the organisation of the text, complete with an index and a remarkable introduction to the origins of the language Esa.

To whom were these translations addressed and what was their genesis? A first answer to the question is found in the introduction to the text quoted above, "*Les noirs peints par eux-mêmes*" from Fr. Bouche. It concerns the first issue of the "*Œuvre de Saint-Jérôme pour la publication des travaux philologiques des missionnaire.*" It was an operation designed to enhance translated texts in order to prevent their disappearance and allow their circulation among those working in Africa.

Considering a significant number of peoples evangelised by the Catholic missionaries, and whose languages are being corrupted or being lost without any serious work left to preserve them for science, several Catholic scholars wondered if it would not be possible to encourage missionaries to print their various observations on the languages of all the countries where they spend more or less long time [...]. Any kind of linguistic work, as their resources would allow, was the best way to realize this project they had been maturing for so long.[7]

The project was an idea of the Marists, who had already started it, but the *Œuvre de Sanit-Jérôme* hoped to be able to count on the contribution of all, The Propaganda Fide contributed to this plan by allowing the distribution of the revenue from the publications between the missions. As you can imagine, the translation work was not an easy task. It was not only a matter of understanding unknown languages, but also of studying and creating an alphabet for languages of oral tradition[8], preparing dictionaries, and translating adequately and usefully for the natives and other missionaries.

This study of the gouro, to my knowledge the first of its kind, succeeds, in short, in identifying the essential features of the phonology and grammar of this language. It provides a useful and comprehensive frame of reference for anyone who would like to learn the gouro [...]. In

---

[7] P. BOUCHE, *Les noirs peints par eux-même*, Paris 1883, I.

[8] G. GUILLET, *Initiation à la tonalité et à la grammaire de la langue Fon*, 1972, typed document, AMA 1N 21, « *Introduction à la méthode: En effet le fongbé ne possède pratiquement aucune littérature écrite mais essentiellement une littérature orale riche en contes, proverbes, chants, prières, louages et devinettes* ».

short, this book offers the researcher a range of interesting materials in such a way that its organisation allows him, at least, to have a synthesis.[9]

A complex commitment, given the meager resources these missionaries had, and the fact that even today there is not yet a complete scientific repertoire of 2, 000 languages in Africa.

As mentioned above, we describe these missionaries as "bridge builders". With their arduous dedication, they managed to build the foundations of communication, without which no activity would have been possible. In ancient times, among the Etruscan people, bridge builders were an almost "sacred" caste honoured as sages for their ability to erect the arch considered almost as an expression of the divine. This tradition reached the Romans for whom the *pontifex maximus* (*pontem* "bridge" and *facĕre* "to do") was the one who supports the religious arch of the care of the deities, as the wedge supports the arch of the bridge.[10]

Thanks to these rudimentary grammar texts that the missionaries created, the first translations of sacred prayers and writings were made, of which the SMA library retains various titles. Among the oldest, there is a small catechism from 1882 in the Yoruba language *Iketuru ti Katikismu* [11]; the *Katekismu e no klon dô, Dan-hô-mê* of 1898 by Fr. Steinmetz mentioned above and a collection of prayers *Yêhue e no ha Kpodo* from 1911.[12]

Nevertheless, there was a criticism of the way in which the first translation works were done. They were criticised for the lack of scientific approach and for being "tainted by a concordance with the missionary's mother tongue."[13] Indirect answers to these judgments can be found in the introductions to the dictionaries composed by the missionaries themselves, where they share witnessing many challenges and pitfalls involved in this task and the awareness of not having many tools at their disposal for the task which was actually essential to their work in Africa.

---

[9] J.P. BENOIST, *Grammaire Gouro, Afrique et langage*, Lyon, typed document, vol I, Lyons 1969, 1.

[10] https://www.romanoimpero.com/2010/06/i-pontefici.html.

[11] *Adura Owuro Ati Alé, Ikekuru ti Katikismu. Orin Mimó, Imprimerie Pitrat Ainé*, Mission du Bénin, Lyons 1882.

[12] *Yêhue e no ha Kpodo. Yêhue han e no ji lê kpan die*, Mission Catholique, Ouidah 1911.

[13] M. HOUIS, *Aperçu sur les structures grammaticales des langues Négro-Africaines (suivi de réflexions sur le langage en Afrique Noire)*, Afrique et langage, 1967, 2.

The study of a language is easier the simpler its alphabet is, and since what we are going to study has no other elements put in writing, we have chosen to use almost exclusively the letters of the French alphabet. [...]. For him [the African person] he learns a language by listening to others speaking, just as one learns a dance by watching others dance [...]. Blacks have learned their mother tongue without ever worrying about the rules that govern it, and they, too, would be very embarrassed to answer you on this subject [...].[14]

Since blacks on the coast of Guinea do not have special characters to write their languages, I will use French characters for this booklet. Sounds or articulations that are not expressed by the letters of our alphabet are represented by punctuated or accented signs and letters of which I approximate the pronunciation below [...].[15]

In 1917, Fr. Joseph Corbeau composed his "First reading book ébé n'o éé n'unu ésa", an alphabet for children learning English, with a few terms and concrete examples of sentences and numbers:

Too often, the small child learning to read English does not understand what he says or is not interested by the form of the sentence. It is to provide a remedy to these inconveniences that we have composed this first reading book [...].[16]

It is clear that it is not the scientific study of language that guided the missionary in writing the text, and this is not the way to read and study their works today. The practical need [17] was the first urgency of the religious. They had to invent and create by themselves and often for the first time, the tools necessary for the accomplishment of their mission. And these tools, at least in the beginning, could only be experimental, rudimentary, and fragile. We know today that documents written by them are a valuable source, a concrete foundation from which one can begin the study of African languages and their evolution.

---

[14] J. JOULORD, *Manuel Français-Dahoméen. Grammaire, phrases usuelles, vocabulaires*, Lyon, Imprimerie vve M. Paquet, 1907, 10, 8.

[15] J.M.J. [sic], *Petits exercices préparatoires pour l'étude de l'Agni*, Papeterie Générale, Imp. Eug. Mercier, Lyons 1901, 5.

[16] J. CORBEAU, *First reading-book ébé n'o éé n'unu èsa*, Imprimerie Armoricaine, Nantes 1917, 1.

[17] J.P. ESCHLIMANN, P. JABOULAY, *Lexique Français-Agni*, typed document : « *Les artisans de ce lexique ne sont nullement des linguistes diplômés et confirmés. C'est par nécessité d'une présence plus vraie et plus intense et d'un meilleur service des ethnies agni dans lesquelles nous travaillons que nous avons entrepris le présent travail [...]* », 1980, 1.

Moreover, and it is not a secondary aspect, these collections could contain expressions, concepts, idioms, cultural traditions and customs that have probably disappeared. The missionaries were well aware of this scenario. In 1970, Fr. Joseph Roth (1917-1985) types a work of his confrere Fr. Antoine Brungard (1897-1961): *Grammaire cabraise* for fear that it could be lost: "Father Brungard's archives have disappeared after his death. But one night in August 1947, taking advantage of an absence, I copied his essay notebooks [...]."[18]

What threatens many African languages today are not the old colonial languages but the other African languages that, for socio-economic reasons, enjoy a higher social status. A language is considered endangered if it is spoken by less than 5, 000 people, has no intergenerational transmission, no social prestige, and there are one or more predominant languages in the same region.[19]

In more elaborate dictionaries, both in manuscripts and in printed materials preserved in the SMA Archives in Rome, often in their introductions there is information on the methodology adopted, the concrete problems, the geographical areas and the populations concerned.[20] These are fundamental details because they concern traditions that have been transformed today by the ongoing development and the influence of other cultures. These aspects had already been emphasised by Fr. Pierre Knops (1898-1986) in the introduction to his *Dictionnaire encyclopédique Français-Senoufo* where he remarked that after 35 years, from the beginning of writing of his dictionary till the end of this work, many things had already changed.

It is during the period between 1923 and 1935 that we got to know the Sénufo, especially those in northern Ivory Coast. The observer who would have visited them recently could see that many social and religious institutions, have evolved or became outdated, and economic changes and progress would no longer allow us to recognize the ancient

---

[18] J. ROTH, *Grammaire cabraise du père Brungard*, AMA 1N 1, Pagouda 1970, 1.
[19] Cf., I. MICHELI, *The natural supremacy of spoken language. Orality and writing in Africa*, in I. Micheli et al. edited by, *Language and identity theories and experiences in lexicography and linguistic policies in a global world*, Trieste 2021, 43-55.
[20] As an example, P. PAGEAUD, l'*Introduction* in *Lexique Beté*, Afrique et Langage, Paris 1972, offers a clear image about what concerns the dialect: the geographical area, population, origins, sub-groups, affinity with other dialects, etc.

reality of this ethnic group [...]. The elements were written before 1935, when the institutions and traditions had their fullest integrity. [21]

The encyclopedic character of this dictionary is the source of a multiplicity of information on the culture and traditions of the Sénufo. The word *fraternity*, for example, is followed by a detailed description of the different meanings of the term, its customs and traditions associated with it: *"According to their ceremonies and public manifestations, two fraternities had the following names, the first nyãra or bangaraga, the next, tyénungo, kwonro, ounayago [...]"*. [22]

In the 1930s, an important innovation was introduced that would transform the *mare magnum* of translations into African languages.

In 1930-1931, African linguists, anxious to transcribe their languages accurately, decided to replace the Latin alphabet, which was inadequate for African languages, with a phonetic alphabet. The transcription system used is that of the International Phonetics Association (IPA) reviewed by the International African Institute (IAI). It allows both to satisfy the scientific rigor and facilitates the rapid literacy of the population. [23]

With this method in 1963, Fr. Basil Segurola (1911-1989) published the *Dictionnaire Fon-Français*. [24] "Since then, it [the work] has been used by all researchers, with a few improvements [...]. The ecumenical translation team of the Bible in Fon decided to use this same scripture and in 1967 the Gospel of St. Mark was published." [25]

At the core of this methodology was also the need for a simple and accurate writing, unlike Latin languages spelling of which is considered very difficult. It was a search to find a definitive way to write according to the pronunciation.

Letters that are not pronounced are not written. Why put a letter h at the end of Ouidah as a city name? A single sound is expressed by the single letter [...]. Each sound must be expressed by its own sign (letter or tone). [26]

---

[21] P. KNOPS, *Dictionnaire encyclopedique Français-Senoufo,* typed document, AMA 1N 34, 1968, 2-3.

[22] P. KNOPS, *Dictionnaire encyclopedique Français-Senoufo*, 130.

[23] G. GUILLET, *Initiation à la tonalité*, 1.

[24] B. SEGUROLA, *Dictionnaire Fon-Français*, Procure de l'Archidiocèse, Cotonou 1963, 2 volls.

[25] G. GUILLET, *Initiation à la tonalité*, 1.

[26] *ibid.*, 2.

To increase the understanding of the value of this background concerning African languages, the SMA Archives in Rome are preparing a project with the collaboration of specialists and professors and, if possible, students, including doctoral students. In the appendix, we offer a first directory of the languages surveyed from the texts in our library. This list, made up of about 50 languages, was developed by Professor Ilaria Micheli[27] basing it on the website *Ethnologue. Languages of the world.*[28]

Lingue/dialetti africani

Adioucrou [ADJ] Alternative names Adyukru, Adjukru, Adyoukrou, Ajuru. Southern Department, Subprefecture of Bonoua, some in Subprefecture of Grand Bassam. Classification: Niger-Congo >Atlantic Congo > Volta-Congo > Kwa > Nyo > Agneby. Autonym: Mɔjukru.

Agni/Bini alternative name for **Anyin** [ANY] (Anyi; Agni). Classification: Niger-Congo >Atlantic Congo > Volta-Congo > Kwa > Nyo > Potou Tano > Tano > Central > Bia > Northern. Dialects: Sanvi, Indenie, Bini, Bona, Mornou, Djuablin; Ano, Abe, Bararbo, Alangua.

Alladian alternative name of **Aladian** [ALD], Aladyan, Alagia, Alagian, Alladyan. Classification: Niger-Congo >Atlantic Congo > Volta-Congo > Kwa > Nyo > Avicam > Aladian.

Angas Alternative name for **Ngas**, Nngas, Kerang, Karang [ANC]. Classification: Afro-Asitic > Chadic > West > A > A3 > Angas Proper. Dialects: Hill Angas; Plain Angas.

Attié (Akye) [ATI] Alternative names: Atie, Akye, Akie; Atche; Atshe. Classification: Niger-Congo >Atlantic Congo > Volta-Congo > Kwa > Nyo > Attie. Dialects: Naindin, Ketin, Bodin.

Baatonum alternative name for **Bariba** [BBA] Other names: Baatonu, Baatombu, Baruba, Bargu, Burgu, Berba, Barba, Bogung, Bargawa, Barganchi. Classification: Niger-Congo >Atlantic Congo > Volta-Congo > North > Gur > Bariba. Dialect: Boko.

Bambara [BRA] alternative names: Bamana, Bamanakan. Classification: Niger-Congo > Mande > Western > Northwestern > Northern > Greater Mandekan > Mandekan > Manding. Dialects: Bamana (Standard Bambara), Dyangirte, kalongo, Masasi, Nyamasa, Soomono, Toro.

---

[27] Professor of Languages and Literature of Africa, Trieste University.
[28] https://www.ethnologue.com/.

Baoulé alternative name for **Baule** [BCI] Alternative names: Bawule. Classification: Niger-Congo >Atlantic Congo > Volta-Congo > Kwa > Njo > Potou Tano > Tano > Central > Bia > Northern.

Bassar alternative name for **Ntcham** [BUD] Alternative names: Basare, Bassari, Basari, Basar, Ncham, Natchamba, Tobote. Classification: Niger-Congo >Atlantic Congo > Volta-Congo > North > Gur > Central > Oti-Volta > Gurma > Ntcham. Dialects: Ncanm, Ntaapum, Ceemba, Linangmanli, all in Togo.

Berem alternative name for **Berom** [BOM]. Alternative names: Birom, Berum, Gbang, Kibo, Kibbo, Kibbun, Kibyen, Shosho, Aboro, Boro-Aboro, Afango, Chenberom. Classification: Niger-Congo >Atlantic Congo > Volta-Congo > Benue Congo > Platoid > Plateau > Southern. Dialects: Gyell-Kuru-Vwang, Fan-Forn-Heikpang, Bachit-Gashish, Du-Ropp-Rim, Hoss.

Cabrais alternative name for **Kabiyè** [KBP] Alternative names: Kabre, Cabrai, Kabure, Kabye. Classification: Niger-Congo > Atlantic Congo > Volta-Congo > North > Gur > Central > Southern > Grusi > Eastern. Dialect: Lama.

Dan [DAF] Alternative names: Yacouba, Yakuba, Da, Gio, Gio-Dan. Classification: Niger-Congo > Mande > Easten > Southeastern > Southern > Kweni-Tura > Tura-Dan-Mano > Tura-Dan. Dialects: Gweetaawu (Eastern Dan), Blowo (Western Dan) + at least other 20 varieties.

Dida: two varieties 1. **Dida Lakota** [DIC]. 2. **Dida Yocoube** [GUD] Alternative names: 1. Dieko, Gabo, Satro, Guebié, Brabori, Ziki. Classification: Niger-Congo > Atlantic Congo > Volta-Congo > Kru > Eastern > Dida. Dialects: Lozoua, Divo + subvarieties.

Djmini Alternative name for **Senoufo**, Djimini [DYI]. Alternative names: Dyimini, Jinmini. Classification: Niger-Congo > Atlantic Congo > Volta-Congo > North > Gur > Senoufo > Tagwana-Djimini. Dialects: Diamala (Djamala, Dyamala), Djafolo, Dofana, Foolo, Singala.

Ebe Alternative name for **Asu** (see online Ethnologue) [AUM]. Classification: Niger-Congo > Atlantic Congo > Volta-Congo > Benue-Congo > Nupoid > Nupe-Gbagyi > Nupe.

Ebrié [EBR] Alternative names: Tyama, Kyama, Tsama, Cama, Caman). Niger-Congo > Atlantic Congo > Volta-Congo > Kwa > Nyo > Potou-Tano > Potou.

Ego; Eggon [EGO] Alternative names: Egon, Megong, Mada, Eggon. Niger-Congo > Atlantic Congo > Volta-Congo > Benue-Congo > Platoid > Plateau > Western > Southwestern > B. Dialects: Matatarwa, Matengala, Hill Mada.

41

Esa alternative name for **Esan** [ISH]. Other names: Ishan, Isa, Anwain. Classification: Niger-Congo > Atlantic Congo > Volta-Congo > Benue-Congo > edoid > North-Central > Edo-Esan-Ora. Dialects: Ekpon, Igueben.

Éwé [EWE] Alternative names: Eibe, Ebwe, Eve, Efe, Eue, Vhe, Gbe, Krepi, Krepe, Popo. Classification: Niger-Congo > Atlantic Congo > Volta-Congo > Kwa > Left Bank > Gbe. Dialects: Anglo, Awuna, Hudu, Kotafoa.

Fanti a dialect of **Akan** [TWS]. Classification: Niger-Congo > Atlantic Congo > Volta-Congo > Kwa > Nyo > Potou-Tano > Tano > Central > Akan. Dialects: Fante (Fanti, Mfantse), Akuapem (Akwapem, twi, akuapim, Akwapi), Asante (Ashante twi, Asanti, Ashanti), Agona, Dankyira, Asen, Akyem, Bosome, kwawu, Ahafo.

Fon alternative name for **Fon-Gbé** [FOA] Alternative names: Fo, Fonnu, Fogbe. Classification: Niger-Congo > Atlantic Congo > Volta-Congo > Kwa > Left Bank > Gbe > Fon. Dialects: Fo, Kotafou.

Ga / Ga-Adangme-Krobo. Alternative names: Amina, Gain, Accra, Acra. Classification: Niger-Congo > Atlantic Congo > Volta-Congo > Kwa > Nyo > Ga-Dangme. Dialects: Ga, Adangme, (Adangbe, Dangle, Dangbe), Krobo.

Gbaraun (Izon) Alternative name for **Ijo**, Central Western. Alternative names: Izon, Izo, Uzo. Classification: Niger-Congo > Atlantic Congo > Ijoid > Ijo > Central, Central Western. Dialects: Iduwini, Ogulagha, Oporoza (Gbaranmatu), Arogbo, Egbema, Olodiama, East Oporoma, Apoi, Gbarain, Kolukuma (Kolokuma, North Izon), Bumo (South Central Izon), ekpetiamap, Ikibiri, Boma, Ogbe Ijo.

Gen-Gbe [GEJ] Alternative names: Ge, Mina-Gen, Mina, Popo, Guin, Gebe. Classification: Niger-Congo > Atlantic Congo > Volta-Congo > Kwa > Left bank > Gbe > Mina.

Goemai [ANK] Alternative names: Anyway, Ankwei, Ankwe, Kemai. Classification: Aro-Asitic > Chadic > West > A > A.3 > Angas Proper > 2.

Goun alternative name for Gun-be [GUW]. Alternative names: Alada, Alada-Gbe, Gun-Alada, Gun, Gun, Gu, Gugbe. Classification: Niger-Congo > Atlantic Congo > Volta-Congo > Kwa > Left Bank > Gbe > Aja.

Gourmantché/Gurmatché alternative names for **Gourmanchéma** [GUX]. Alternative names: Gourma, Gurma, Goulimanchema. Classification: Niger-Congo > Atlantic Congo > Volta-Congo > North > Gur > Central > Northern > Oti-Volta > Gurma.

Gouro alternative name for **Guro** [GOA] Alternative names: Kweni, Lo, Kwéndré. Classification: Niger-Congo > Mande > Eastern > Southeastern > Southern > Kweni-Tura > Kweni-Yaoure.

Gworok Alternative name for **Tyap** [KCG]. A language of Nigeria. Classification: Niger-Congo > Atlantic Congo > Volta-Congo > Benue-Congo > Plateau > Central > South-Central (only online version).

Haoussa/Hausa [HUA] Alternative names: Hausawa, Abakwariga, Mgbakpa, Habe, Karo. Classification: Afro-Asiatic > Chadic > West > A > A.1. Dialects: Eastern Hausa, Western Hausa, North Hausa.

Ibo alternative name for **Igbo** [IGR]. 1995. Classification: Niger-Congo > Atlantic Congo > Volta-Congo > Benue-Congo > Igboid > Igbo. Dialects: Owerri (Isuama), Onitsha, Umuahia (Ohuhu), Orlu, Ngwa, Afikpo, Nsa, Okuta, Aniocha, Eche, Egbema.

Kagoro [XKG] Alternative name Kakolo. Classification: Niger-Congo > Mande > Wesrtern > Northwestern > Northern > Greater Mandekan > Mandekan > Manding. Warning: kagoro seems also to be an alternative name for Tyap (see Gworok).

Kekere? Alternative name for Kerebe [KED] Tanzania? Alternative names Ekikerebe, Kerewe. Classification: Niger-Congo > Atlantic Congo > Volta-Congo > Benue-Congo > Bantoid > Southern > Narrow bantu > Central > J > Haya-Jita (J. 20).

Kotokoli alternative name for **Tem** [KDH] Alternative names: Cotocoli, Tim, Time, Temba. Classification: Niger-Congo > Atlantic Congo > Volta-Congo > > North > Gur > Central > Southern > Grusi > Eastern.

Kukuruku [ETS] Alternative name for **Etsako**. A language of Nigeria. Classification: Niger-Congo > Atlantic Congo > Volta-Congo > Benue-Congo > Edoid > North-Central > Gothuo-Uneme-Yekhee. Only online version.

Kulango (Koulango) Bondoukou + Bouna [KZC and NKU]. Classification: Niger-Congo > Atlantic Congo > Volta-Congo > North > Gur > Kulango. Dialect Nabanj.

Lelemi [LEF] Alternative names: Lefana, Lafana, Buem. Classification: Niger-Congo > Atlantic Congo > Volta-Congo > Kwa > Nyo > Potou-Tano > Lelemi > Lelemi-Akpafu.

Lolobi alternative name for **Siwu** [AKP] Classification: Niger-Congo > Atlantic Congo > Volta-Congo > Kwa > Nyo > Potou-Tano > Lelemi > Lelemi-Akpafu - strongly related to Lelemi.

Mandyak [MFV] Alternative names: Mandjaque, Manjaca, manjaco, Manjiak, Kanyop, Manjaku, Manjack, Ndyak, Mendyako).

Classification: Niger-Congo > Atlantic Congo > Atlantic > Northern > Bak > Manjaku-Papel. Dialects. Bok (Babok, Sarar, Teixeira Pinto, Tsaam), Likes-Utsia (Baraa, Kalkus), Cur (Churo), Lund, Yu (Pecixe, Siis, Pulhilh).

Moba [MFQ] Alternative names: Moab, Moare, Moa, Ben. Classification: Niger-Congo > Atlantic Congo > Volta-Congo > North > Gur > Central > Northern > Oti-Volta > Burma > Moba. Dialect: Natchaba.

Mossi alternative name for **Mòoré** [MHM] Alternative names: Mosse, More, Mole, Moshi. Classification: Niger-Congo > Atlantic Congo > Volta-Congo > North > Gur > Central > Northern > Oti-Volta > Western > Northwest. Dialects: Saramdé, Taolendé, Yaadré, Oupadoupou, Yaande, Zaore (Joore).

Nago - Northern - Southern [NQG] Alternative names: Nagots, Nagot, Ede Nago. Classification: Niger-Congo > Atlantic Congo > Volta-Congo > Benue-Congo > Defoid > Yoruboid > Edekiri.

Nkwizi impossible to refer the label to any known language. Further investigation needed.

Nzema [NZE] Alternative names Nzima, Appolo. Classification: Niger-Congo > Atlantic Congo > Volta-Congo > Kwa > Nyo > Potou-Tano > tano > Central > Bia > Southern.

Peulh (Fulfulde) /Peul alternative name for **Fulfulde** [FUV] alternative names: Kano-Katsina-Bororro.

Sango [SAJ] + Sango Riverain [SNJ]. Alternative name: Shango. Classification: Niger-Congo > Atlantic Congo > Volta-Congo > Benue-Congo > Bantoid > Southern > Narrow Bantu > Central > G > Bena-Kinga (G.61).

Senoufo/Senufo - Senufo is actually a continuum comprising different variants in Burkina Faso - Ivory Coast (S. Nanerigé, S. Niangolo. S. Sìcíte in BF and S. Cebaara, S. Djimini - see Djimini above - S. Niarafolo-Niafolo, S. Palaka, S. Shempire, S. Taiwan - Tagbana, Tagwana, Tagouna - in IC). Classification: Niger-Congo > Atlantic Congo > Volta-Congo > North > Gur > Senufo > different variants.

Tagbana see **Senoufo.**

Tagwana see **Senoufo.**

Toura [NEB] Alternative names: Tura, Ween. Classification: Niger-Congo > Mande > Eastern > Southeastern >Southern > Kweni-Toura > Tura-Dan-Mano > Tura-Dan. Dialects: Naò, Boo, Yiligele, Gwéò, Wáádú.

Yacouba see **Dan** above.

Yom [PIL]. A language of Benin. Classification: Niger-Congo > Atlantic Congo > Volta-Congo > North > Gur > Central > Northern > Oti-Volta > Yom-Nawdm. Just online version.

Yombe [YOM] Alternative names: Kiyombe, kiombi, Bayombe). Dialects: Mbala (Mombala), Vungunya (kivungunya, Yombe classique). A language of the Democratic Republic of the Congo. Classification: Niger-Congo > Atlantic Congo > Volta-Congo > bene-Congo > Bantoid > Southern > Narrow Bantu > Central > H > Kikongo (H.16).

Yoruba [YOR] Alternative names: Yooba, Yariba. Dialects: oyo, Ijesha, Ila, Ijebu, Ondo, Wo, Owe, Jumu, Iworro, Igbena, yagba, gbedde, egba, Akono, Aworo, Bunu (Bini), Ekiti, Ilaje, Ikale, Awori. Classification: Niger-Congo > Atlantic Congo > Volta-Congo > Benue-Congo > Defoid > Yoruboid > Edekiri.

Connecting with the Coptic Church

Vilsan Kodavatikanti SMA

The SMA has been in Egypt since November 1877 when Fathers Duret and Le Gallen landed in Alexandria and reported to the Apostolic Vicar of Alexandria, Mgr. Ciurcia. They were both sent to Zagazig in Egypt. Father Jacob Muyser, with his contribution to Coptic liturgy, changed the missionary dynamics of the SMA in Egypt with consequences that last until today. He dedicated his life to the Egyptian Coptic church and espoused the cause of its unity through the renewal of Coptic liturgy. Thus, he was called the Apostle of Unity in Egypt. Mgr. Youhanna Kabes, the Patriarch of the Coptic Catholic Church wrote to Fr. Gerard Viaud SMA, who was the parish priest of Facous in Egypt, describing Fr. Jacob Muyser, saying "He was attached to the tradition he knew and loved so well. He recognised its value and its riches and affirmed in his lectures and his writings, to all the missionaries of Egypt, that the liturgy was a point of capital importance for the Apostolate. It was the common ground, the solid ground, the starting point for the unity of the Copts." [1] Jacob Muyser was a unifying influence in the Coptic Church, especially in the field of liturgy, through his scholarly research and writings and

---

[1] G. VIAUD, *La Bibliograghie du Qommos Jacob Muyser*, Cairo 1966. « Il s'attacha à la tradition qu'il a si bien connue et aimée. Il a reconnu sa valeur et ses richesses et affirma dans ses conférences et ses écrits, à tous les missionnaires d'Égypte, que la liturgie est un point d'une importance capitale pour l'Apostolat. C'est le terrain commun, le terrain solide le point de départ pour l'Unité des Coptes. »

his passionate pastoral ministry. This great missionary who, through his endeavours, forged an exceptional link between the SMA and the Church, deserves to be better known.

Early life

Jacob Louis Lambert Muyser was born in The Hague, Holland, on May 9, 1896. He was the eldest son of Jacob John Marcus Egbertus Muyser and Henrietta Antonia Maria Beernink. His father was the financial secretary to Her Majesty Queen Wilhelmina of Holland. The first years of Jacob Muyser's life were happy and carefree. He had a very generous disposition and shared easily whatever he received. He began his studies at the primary school of the Brothers of the Immaculate Conception where he was one the most studious pupils. The first pain in the life of Jacques Muyser was caused by the death of his mother on October 15, 1901. Jacques (the name he used at home) continued his studies at the Brothers of the College of Saint-Louis of Rurmonde. In this college, at the age of twelve, he received his First Holy Communion in the month of May, 1908. Jacques was distinguished in the school by his intelligence and exemplary piety. From 1908 on Jacques' academic career continued at Katwijk College, Nijmegen College and Willibrordus College, all run by the Jesuit Fathers. He was known for his seriousness, his curiosity and love for studies. During his college years Jacques showed great religious zeal and a particular gift for languages, Along with his passion for study he was also very interested in the social and political events of Holland. He often went to Parliament to follow members' debates. On the final day of "mission" organised in his College on June 21, 1915, he was touched by the enthusiastic sermon of one Jesuit priest. From that moment, Jacques was certain of his vocation and was determined to become a missionary and preferably in Africa.[2]

The missionary vocation

Returning home, Jacques Muyser informed his family of his decision. They were very surprised and could not believe in this sudden vocation. A month after graduating from high school, he joined the Nobertin Fathers of Heeswijk Abbey to improve his knowledge of classical languages. He remained there for a year then was admitted, in 1916, to

---

[2] G. VIAUD, *Le Qommos Jacob Muyser, Apôtre de l'Unité en Terre de Gessen*, Cairo 1996 1-3.

the house of Saint Charles of Boxtel of the White Fathers of Cardinal Lavigerie for his novitiate. There he studied philosophy, began his theological studies and undertook the study of the Arabic language. But in 1918, learning that for medical reasons he could not go to Africa, Jacques was very disappointed. Disturbed, but not discouraged, Jacques left the White Fathers and entered the University of Fribourg in Switzerland, where for a year (1918-1919) he devoted himself to ecclesiastical studies. Tenacious and never allowing himself to be discouraged by difficulties, he left the University of Fribourg to enter the Society of African Missions in Lyons towards the end of the year 1919.[3]

Beginning of the new Coptic Mission and its adaptation

On October 18, 1919, Jacques Muyser began his novitiate at the African Missions in Lyons in order to leave for Africa. During his first months in the novitiate, he and many other seminarians were affected by an epidemic of dysentery. It was during this illness that he met the first Egyptian, Alexander Scandar, who was a nurse at the seminary. Later, they collaborated together in Egypt and Alexander Scandar became the Catholic Coptic Bishop of Assiut.

One day, Father Chabert, a former missionary in Egypt and superior general of the SMA, entered Jacques Muyser's room to ask him for information about the University of Fribourg. He saw an Arabic grammar book and a dictionary on the table and realised that he knew a bit of Arabic. He decided to send him to Egypt. In 1919, the SMA was addressing the problem of the apostolate among the Copts in Egypt.[4]

---

[3] *Ibid.*, 4-5.

[4] The Copts who are the direct descendants of the Egyptians of pharaonic Egypt. The word Coptic is only the abbreviation, by the suppression of the initial diphthong, of "aiguptos," a Greek term for Egypt. The word Coptic therefore designates a people, a language (that which was spoken in ancient Egypt and which was transcribed in Greek characters with seven complementary letters), an art, a literature, a calendar (with 12 months of 30 days and one additional month of 5 to 6 days) and a very special liturgy. The Church of Egypt, of which the Copts are the heirs, was founded by Saint Mark in Alexandria where he was martyred in 68. This Church separated from the rest of Byzantine and Latin Christianity at the Council of Chalcedon in 451 as a result of the verbal quarrel about the person of Christ and his two natures. This church, born in Alexandria, first used the Greek language and from the fourth century the liturgical books and the Bible were translated into Coptic. Since the

This apostolate was then considered, according to the ideas of the time, to involve the conversion of Orthodox Copts to Catholicism. Without even having completed six months of novitiate, Jacques Muyser got ready to embark for Egypt. In a letter of July 6, 1920, Father Chabert wrote to Father Pagès, superior of the SMA in Egypt: "Mr. Muyser is a person of great value... I would like you to place him immediately in an Arabic environment; he is destined for the mission to the Copts ". Thus, Father Pagès appointed him to the Zagazig mission.[5]

Arrival in Egypt

On August 28, 1920, Father Muyser embarked for Egypt and arrived in Alexandria on September 5th. In a first letter to the Superior General, which he wrote from Zagazig on September 14, 1920, Father Muyser described his first impressions of Egypt:

"Here I am on September 13 (in Zagazig) with Father Pagès in the Promised Land or rather in the land of Goshen, of Joseph and Jacob... (I) devoted all my time to the private study of Arabic and speaking with the little Arab children short sentences in Arabic... Currently we are looking for an English teacher... I do not know what to follow and in which direction to go. I forge ahead with the help of God. I do not underestimate either the enormous difficulties, or the lengthy self-preparation for Arabic and the idea of working probably only for the benefit of a future generation. Here the opinion, from what I hear in general, is that it is a long-term endeavour, extremely delicate and one in which we cannot advance quickly. In short, as I move on experience will guide me better as to the method to follow, the paths to take..."[6]

---

eleven century, all these books have been translated into Arabic. Today, the liturgy is celebrated in both Coptic and Arabic languages.
[5] G. VIAUD, *Le Qommos Jacob Muyser, Apôtre de l'Unité en Terre de Gessen,* 5.
[6] *Ibid.,* 8. (Original french text) « Me voici le 13 septembre (à Zagazig) avec le Père Pagès en terre promise ou plutôt en terre de Goshen, de Joseph et de Jacob... (Je) consacrais tout mon temps à l'étude privée de l'arabe et à parler avec le petits enfants arabes phrases courtes en arabe... Actuellement nous recherchons un professeur d'anglais... Je ne sais pas à quoi adhérer et dans quelle direction j'avance avec l'aide de Dieu. Je ne sais pas, ni les énormes difficultés, ni la longue préparation de soi pour l'arabe et l'idée de travailler probablement seulement pour une génération future. Ici, l'opinion, d'après ce que j'entends en général, est qu'il s'agit d'une entreprise à long terme, extrêmement délicate et dans laquelle nous ne pouvons pas marcher Bref,

In his letter, Father Muyser went on to talk about the Coptic village at the bottom of the Zagazig Mission Garden.

"There are about thirteen families living there, Orthodox Copts and Catholics... Everything is crowded. There is everything, pigeons, chickens, donkeys and a lot of dirt that disgusts you at first sight and your reactions must be controlled day by day.... I go every day to the village to have a chat with everyone... I hope to be able to have close contact with these people in order to do some good there. I intend to write a little bit about the Copts in a Dutch missionary magazine to raise awareness about them."[7]

Coptic liturgy and SMA missionaries

There are three liturgies used in the Coptic Orthodox and Coptic Catholic Churches and they are almost identical for both denominations. Jacob Muyser was able to carry out research into the liturgy by studying the ancient Coptic manuscripts. Eventually he became one of the most important experts in the Coptic Church not only for Coptic Catholics but also for Orthodox scholars. Thus, whenever someone writes about the Orthodox and Catholic ecumenical dialogue they refer to Father Jacob Muyser. Fr. Aubert speaking about the unity of Coptic Orthodox and Catholics in his article "The Educator, The Instigator of the union of the Copts" refers to Jacob Muyser saying "Qommos Jacob Muyser remarked in his article *"Rayon D'Egypte"* on 13 January 1952 that nothing suggests a possible agreement between Rome and the separated Oriental Churches, that it needs a slow and long preparation."[8] Usually the Coptic liturgy is composed of

The Liturgy according to St Basil, Bishop of Caesarea

---

l'expérience me guidera mieux, au fur et à mesure, sur la méthode à suivre, les moyens à prendre... »

[7] *Ibid.* (The original french text) « Il y a environ treize familles qui vivent là-bas, des coptes orthodoxes et des catholiques... Tout est surpeuplé. Il y a de tout, des pigeons, des poules, des ânes et beaucoup de saletés qui vous dégoûtent au premier instant et doivent être contrôlées au jour le jour.... Je vais tous les jours au village pour bavarder avec chacun... J'espère que je pourrais avoir des contacts intimes avec ces gens pour y faire du bien... Je compte écrire un peu sur les Coptes dans un missionnaire hollandais magazine pour les sensibiliser. »

[8] « L'Educateur Instrument D'union des Copte » in *Les Cahiers Copte, Institut Copte*, Vol. No. I, Cairo 1952, 20.

The Liturgy according to St Gregory of Nazianzus, Bishop of Constantinople

The Liturgy according to St Cyril I, the 24th Patriarch of the Coptic Orthodox Church

The Liturgy according to St. Basil is the one used most of the year; St. Gregory's Liturgy is used during the feasts and on certain occasions; only parts of St. Cyril's Liturgy are used nowadays. It is worth noting here that the Liturgy was first used (orally) in Alexandria by St. Mark and that it was recorded in writing by St. Cyril I, the 24th Patriarch of the Coptic Orthodox Church of Egypt. This is the Liturgy known as St. Cyril's Liturgy and from which the other two liturgies, referred to above, are derived. These liturgies are available in Arabic and in the ancient Coptic language though Arabic is more prevalent as the Coptic language is practically extinct. They include lengthy prayers, which make the celebrations rather long. The whole liturgy involves a lot of Coptic chanting which makes it lively, solemn and participatory.

No SMA missionary in Egypt had adopted the Coptic rite to facilitate his apostolate. In Zagazig, there was a group of SMA Fathers and among them was a distinguished Arabic scholar Father Laroche. The superiors then thought of using the knowledge and zeal of Father Laroche in the parish ministry of the Coptic faithful who were without a priest. But he was of the Latin rite and it seemed impossible then to accustom the new Coptic parishioners to the ceremonies of the Roman liturgy.

Jacob Muyser arrived in Egypt with one desire: to devote himself totally to the work of the unity of the Church by travelling along the path that separated the Eastern Catholics from their brethren in terms of rites and traditions. He would become one of the pioneers of ecumenism. Settled in Zagazig, the young seminarian completed his studies of theology while continuing the study of Arabic. His free time was devoted to caring for the few Coptic families settled in the village created by the Fathers in the garden of the mission. Every evening, he gathered these Christians to teach them catechism and to have them pray, all in keeping with his progress in the Arabic language.

On October 10, 1920, Jacques Muyser made his oath in Cairo to belong to the SMA, only two months after his arrival in Egypt. On this occasion he received the tonsure and the four minor orders. In December 1920, Father Girard wrote to the superior general: "In Zagazig, Mr. Muyser is doing very well. He is already starting to get in touch with the Copts of the village and even with some in the city... I was pleasantly surprised by the progress he has made in Arabic ".[9] At the beginning of the year 1921, Jacques Muyser went to Alexandria to receive Holy Orders. At that time there was no Apostolic Vicar for the Nile Delta, Mgr Duret having not yet been replaced. It was therefore the Latin bishop of Alexandria and Apostolic Delegate, Bishop Brianti, who conferred on him the sacred orders.

Contribution to the Coptic Church

On February 6, 1921, Jacques Muyser was ordained sub deacon, then deacon on February 13 and priest on February 20. Now called Abuna Yacoub, the young priest began his apostolic life. For thirty-four years he followed this apostolic endeavour joined to a life of prayer, study and research. In all the villages where there were Christians, in the Eastern Delta province, Abuna Muyser announced the Good News, taught catechism, listened to people and gave them advice.

A man of few words, he concentrated totally on his studies, his projects and his apostolic concerns, to the point of forgetting to eat and sleep. He was not dogmatic nor a moralizer. He avoided all vain discussion and was very sensitive to being contradicted. He lived in total poverty and detached from worldly concerns. The faith of Father Muyser was unshakeable, bordering on mysticism, and he enlivened it throughout his life by the recitation of the Office, his meditations, the long Coptic ceremonies, and his many contacts with his people and all those he encountered in the course of his research that never took precedence over his pastoral ministry which was essential for him. Everyone who knew Abuna Muyser considered him a saint.

Passionate in pastoral ministry at Facous

It was in May 1921 that Father Muyser went to Facous for the first time. He lived in a rented house on the edge of the railway line from Facous to Salheya. On the ground floor, he opened a primary school and taught catechism along with other subjects. Father Muyser had his apartment upstairs. He spent his summer evenings on the balcony chatting with his guests or dreaming about the future. When Father Muyser built the church, he dedicated it to St. Pachomius, the founder of Egyptian monasticism in the fourth century. He designed it in perfect harmony with the Coptic tradition. Having learned about the Coptic liturgy, he

---

[9] G. VIAUD, *Le Qommos Jacob Muyser, Apôtre de l'Unité en Terre de Gessen*, 20.

did it perfectly. The length of the liturgical celebrations never discouraged him. On the contrary, the longer it was, the more beautiful it was for him, and also for his followers, at least in their great majority.

One day, King Farouk passed by Facous and asked Father Muyser to come and guide him through the ruins of Tanis, an ancient Pharaonic city. Father Muyser was celebrating a service and so he replied: "I am at the service of the King of Kings, so tell King Farouk to wait a little while I finish this service." And King Farouk waited. It shows his pastoral zeal and his conviction.

The successor to Father Muyser at Facous, Father Zakaria Remiro, wrote: "There is, thanks to dear Abuna Yacoub, in Facous a unique Christian atmosphere: our faithful are well prepared to understand and love their priest...".[10]

A man of relationship and a scholar

For Father Muyser, all contact and all relationships seemed to him to be useful and occupied him entirely. He could seem to waste his time in these long conversations. He was interested in the person in front of him, whether he was a school inspector or an antiquities officer, or a poor peasant from the neighbourhood. Thus, he was invariably affable and always welcoming to both Christians and Muslims. Among the latter, he had many friends. He was a man of the people, always placing himself at the level of his interlocutor.

Father Muyser very quickly understood that any apostolate in a civilisation as old as Egypt required a slow and progressive knowledge of the environment, the mentality, the customs and also the religion of ancient Egypt. In his research, he was very methodical, providing notes on the margins of his books and journals, writing on small pieces of paper his reflections or references that he could find and writing his articles on large striped pages in a beautiful script, whether in French, Coptic or Arabic. Moreover, his great general knowledge, which he had acquired, helped him considerably in his work. In his book *"Facing the Coptic Apostolate"*, published in Alexandria in 1950, Father Muyser presented his ideas on apostolic preparation, including the study of Arabic and Coptic languages, the need for specialisation in one of the fields of the Coptic world and skills in adaptation. He says "I look closely at the past to discover lessons. I question the past to better orient myself towards a future apostolate. I hold on to tradition, a common basis, the

---

[10] *Ibid.*, 20.

better to repair broken links. I take a few steps back, the better to move forward."[11] Thus in his scientific research in *"Coptology"* he touched on almost all the areas of studies such as *linguistics, art, archaeology, history, Iconography, Monasticism, liturgy, geography* etc. In many of the published bulletins there was a special column where Jacob Muyser's bibliography was recommended.[12]

His writings attracted the attention of the Coptic Orthodox hierarchy, and he gained their trust through a recognition of his competence. He was often asked for his opinion on historical questions, on Coptic manuscripts, on tradition. His fame became global and he was consulted by a large number of scholars from all over the world.

Two things seemed to him essential: a well-prepared liturgy and the renewal of monasticism among Catholics. He wrote:

"I envisage the establishment of a sound liturgy respecting the living traditions of the Coptic Church and the Coptic people. These traditions date back many centuries and reflect the Coptic soul and its religious spirit, traditions to which the majority of Copts are attached. It is in the interest and the spirit of the Catholic Church everywhere that it develops its high mission to adapt to these traditions and not to destroy them, change them or modernize them".[13]

On July 3, 1945, the administrator of the Catholic Coptic Patriarchate, Mgr. Morcos Khouzam, was in Facous to raise Father Muyser to the hegumenate.[14] He reluctantly accepted this honour. Father Aupiais, then Provincial of the African Missions in Lyons, was

---

[11] G. VIAUD, *La Bibliograghie du Qommos Jacob Muyser*, 4. (The original french text) « Je regarde de près le passé pour en découvrir des leçons. Je questionne le passé pour mieux m'orienter vers un futur apostolat. Je m'accroche à la tradition, un socle commun, pour mieux réparer les liens rompus. Je recule de quelques pas pour mieux avancer »

[12] Livre à consulter, dans : *Bulletin Religieux D'Egypte,* Cairo 1962, I, 14- 16, et II, 13-15.

[13] G. VIAUD, *Le Qommos Jacob Muyser, Apôtre de l'Unité en Terre de Gessen,* 20.(The original french text) « J'envisage la mise en place d'une liturgie saine respectant les traditions vivantes de l'Église copte et du peuple copte. Ces traditions remontent à plusieurs siècles et reflètent l'âme copte et son esprit religieux, traditions auxquelles la majorité des coptes sont attachés. dans l'intérêt et l'esprit de l'Église catholique partout où elle développe sa haute mission de s'adapter à ces traditions et non de les détruire, les changer ou les moderniser »

[14] Hegumenate in the Coptic Church is an order between the priesthood and the episcopate. Igumen, or qommos, is more an honorific title than a function.

present at this ceremony and in his homily on the occasion thus described this vocation:

"Everyone can understand that this generous plan, proposed by the superiors of the African Missions to the Catholic Coptic hierarchy, greatly exceeded the proportions of an ordinary act of sacerdotal zeal. Indeed, the young missionary who had left his homeland and family in the name of his vocation, made an even greater sacrifice by renouncing the rite of his future priesthood, the ceremonies and traditions that had embellished and charmed his childhood and youth. The young missionary, in answering this call, embodied, by this sacrifice, the tender affection and the touching solicitude of Rome with regard to Oriental rites inherited from the apostolic age. Finally, the young missionary made it clear to his future parishioners that Christianity is too big to be confined within the borders of a people, a language or customs". [15]

The end of an apostle of unity

In 1956, Qommos Yacoub Muyser went to Vienna to participate in the 8th Congress of Papyrology. At the end of this Congress, Qommos Yacoub Muyser stopped in Rome to review and make the necessary corrections to the Missal and the ritual of the Coptic Catholic Community then in print at the Papal Printing Office. He stayed at the SMA Generalate. However, he was very tired due to a cancer that had been spreading in his lungs for several months. His soul departed on the morning of April 16, 1956 and he was buried in the concession of the SMA at Campo Verano in Rome near the Basilica of Saint Lawrence.

---

[15] G. VIAUD, *Le Qommos Jacob Muyser, Apôtre de l'Unité en Terre de Gessen*, 23. (The original french text) « Chacun peut comprendre que ce dessin généreux, proposé par les supérieurs des Missions africaines à la hiérarchie copte catholique, dépassait largement les proportions d'un acte ordinaire de zèle sacerdotal. En effet, le jeune missionnaire qui avait quitté sa patrie et sa famille au nom de sa vocation, fit un sacrifice encore plus grand en renonçant au rite de son futur sacerdoce, aux cérémonies et traditions qui avaient embelli et charmé son enfance et sa jeunesse. Le jeune missionnaire, en répondant à cet appel, matérialisait, par ce sacrifice, la tendre affection et la touchante sollicitude de Rome à l'égard des rites orientaux hérités de l'âge apostolique. Enfin, le jeune missionnaire a fait comprendre à ses futurs paroissiens que le christianisme est trop grand pour être confiné dans les frontières d'un peuple, d'une langue ou de coutumes. »

Mission continues in Upper Egypt

The life of Qommos Jacob Muyser, his works, his spirituality and his love for Egypt have left important marks on the presence of the SMA in Egypt since his arrival in 1920. Today, the SMA resumes this missionary orientation with the opening of a ministry to the Coptic people in the Diocese of Sohag. Father Jacob Muyser gives us the necessary and very contemporary guides and tools with which our young missionaries can realize their missionary potential in the service of the people of God. The long-awaited dream of a Mission in Upper Egypt was finally realised in 2017 September 15 with the nomination of two SMA missionaries Fr. John Paul Silué (Ivory Coast) and Fr. Vilsan Kodavatikanti (India) to the Coptic diocese called Sohag. After three long years of discussion between the SMA through the then Delegate Superior Fr. Robbin Kamamba (Kenya) and Mgr.Youssef Aboul Kheir, the Bishop of Sohag welcomed us with open arms. He gave us a residence in a town called Tahta for the first two years and later a parish in a village called Cheikh Zein el Dheen. It contains 20 families and attached to our residence is a building which we use as a youth centre.

Pastoral ministry and adaptation

Egypt is the land of civilisation, the land of inters- religious dialogue with Muslims who constitute 80% of the country's population and also the place of ecumenism due to the presence of the majority of the Coptic Orthodox Church and also various other Christian denominations. Thus, there is great scope for the young missionaries to have a pastoral experience in the Coptic context. In the words of Qommos Jacob Muyser emphasis is rightly placed on missionary adaptation saying

"How ought we be prepared and ready to adapt to specific environments with an already existing Christian organisation, culture, past, and heritage? This is the big question. Adapting to the mission means living better acting better, making oneself more accessible to others. In terms of our apostolate this means making our testimony more accessible, more meaningful, and giving it the opportunity to be heard wherever we are sent." [16]

---

[16] J. MUYSER, « La Relligieuse parmi les Coptes L'Indispensable et L'Ideal » Cairo 1951, 24. (Original french text) « Comment devrions-nous être qualifiés et adaptés à des environnements spécifiques déjà avec une organisation, une culture, un passé et un héritage chrétiens existants? Voici la grande question,

We SMA missionaries faced various challenges in order to adapt to the Coptic liturgy, and to live among the Muslims and Orthodox Christians but these only enriched our pastoral missionary zeal and strengthened our faith as Catholic priests and as Christians, especially in the diocese of Sohag.

Mission challenges

The Arabic Language: For any missionary language is the key to enter the hearts of the people. The classical Arabic which we learnt in college is used for liturgy, for reading books and in academic settings but to speak with the Egyptian people we needed to learn the Egyptian dialect of Arabic which is different from the classical standard Arabic. We had to begin from zero to learn this dialect by talking to the local people. Thanks be to God we were able to give homilies at the end of the year and listen to Confessions in their Egyptian dialect. It was a real challenge.

The Coptic Rite: The sacraments in the Coptic Catholic liturgy are different from those of the Latin rite and contain lot of chanting and lengthy prayers that we were obliged to learn and practise. The parish priests of our respective parishes helped us to learn the chanting and to administer the sacraments appropriately. In this way we learned how to celebrate the Coptic liturgy and to pray with the people. We are proud that one of our SMA Priest Fr. Jacob Muyser contributed to this renewal of the Coptic liturgy.

Evangelisation of the Muslims: Evangelisation and conversion to another religion is strictly prohibited in Egyptian law. Moreover, encountering some radical Muslim groups needs a lot of courage. In the beginning it was a great challenge for us even to greet them. Gradually we were able to make friends with the Muslims around our mission. We were proclaiming the Word through our life of friendship and charity.

Fruits of our missionary work

Deep faith and participation of the faithful and youth in the liturgy: In our four years of ministry, we undertook our pastoral work not only in the SMA parish but also in all the other parishes that needed our help.

---

s'adapter à la mission c'est : mieux vivre mieux agir se rendre plus accessible aux autres. pour notre apostolat, cela signifie rendre notre témoignage plus accessible, plus significatif, et lui donner la chance d'être entendu là où nous sommes envoyés. »

We were also given responsibilities at diocesan level, For instance I was the diocesan youth coordinator and in charge of the choir, and Fr. John Paul Silue was actively participating in missionary vocations. We were really impressed by the deep faith of the faithful and particularly of the Catholic and Orthodox youth. They were so serious in fasting and prayer and their confessions. I was very glad to listen to and counsel them. The faithful generally respect the priests so much that they call us *Qudus Abuna* meaning Our Holy Father.

Cultural Unity: All Egyptians share the same culture and food habits, especially in the villages. One cannot find out whether someone is Muslim or Christian by their dress or work. Because they prepare the same food they celebrate some common festivals together, for instance *sham el Naseem*.[17] I would say that the Egyptian culture unites them so that they live as brothers and sisters. We as young missionaries adopted their way of eating and participating in their feasts to be one with them and to preach Christ through our way of life.

Ecumenical and Inter-religious Dialogue: It is worth mentioning that ecumenical and the inter-religious dialogue is badly needed at the present time in the world as a whole and particularly in Egypt. Given that the very nature of the Church here is ecumenical. our mission demands that we make every effort to promote ecumenical and the interreligious dialogue. In the name of religion, as we are all aware, violent incidents take place from time to time. Generally, the victims are innocent people. As a result, feelings of hatred grow in the minds and hearts of the people. If we allow this to take root, there can never be peace in Egypt. In such a scenario we actively promote a collaborative and practical lifestyle that is deeply embedded in the love of neighbour as taught by Christ. I feel challenged and privileged to share in this ministry of dialogue through various activities in which our parish priest and myself participate and which create opportunities for dialogue with the Orthodox Christians and Muslims living around us. We make use of birth rituals, marriage ceremonies and the three days mourning which are all common to both Christians and Muslims where they meet and share deeply in different life mysteries that surpass human understanding. Whenever these events occur, we go and express

---

[17] This is the feast celebrated just the next day to the Easter, it is the national feast celebrated by all Egyptians irrespective of the religion. On this day people eat a special dish called Muluha which is a kind of pickled fish, and colored eggs. The tradition says that this is a feast that is pharaonic.

our joy or sorrow and through our presence we bring across the message that we are all children of God walking through the same world, the one God who created all human beings. There is always so much mutual respect and appreciation from the Orthodox and Muslim leaders and people when we show our solidarity with them. We also continue to show the love of Christ in the streets when we meet a Muslim or Orthodox cleric by a warm embrace and the exchange of a few words. In this way we are promoting peace and togetherness among the Muslims and Christians so that they can love one another as brothers and sisters. So, in summary, ecumenical and inter-religious dialogue is not only in books and seminars, it is real here and despite the challenges, it works. We open our SMA youth centre not only for the youths of the Catholic diocese but also to the Orthodox and Muslim groups for them to organize seminars and workshops thus promoting unity. During times of crisis we help in looking after the poor of the Muslim and Orthodox faiths as well as the Catholics thus showing our solidarity as Jesus commanded his disciples to do: "Love one another as I loved you."

Conclusion

After having installed the SMA in Sohag diocese in January 2018, Mgr. Yousef Abu al-Khrair, then Bishop of the Sohag Coptic diocese, said, "The SMA Mission in Upper Egypt brings newness and freshness in the diocese of Sohag. The missionary presence adds dynamism to the pastoral work. The presence of foreign missionaries makes the people of God aware of the nature of the Catholic church as universal and missionary". The truth of this is clear from the way the people received us and share their lives with us. It is also evident through the lives of our great missionaries We are slowly overcoming the various challenges such as mastering the Arabic language, learning the Coptic Rite, administering the Sacraments and adapting to the Egyptian culture and traditions of the people. There is no conversion to religion here as it is forbidden by law. But the SMA is sharing its missionary light by bringing a new spirit to the mission and life of the church in Upper Egypt. The Christians here are now realising the Church is more than the Diocese of Sohag, it is missionary, and we hope this will help in making Christ known and loved in a deeper way through our humble presence here.

Our Vision

Let us not leave out the traditional leaders

Dominic Xavier Vincent SMA

Summary: Traditional leaders have a predominant place among the Baatombu. Despite the rapid progress in the socio-political and economic sphere, how do they maintain such influence over their society? Although feudalism has been officially rejected, how is it still practiced? What is the foundation of the traditional authority? The history of the Nikki kingdom reveals many factors that have weakened the sovereignty of the kings. Nonetheless, in the socio-cultural and traditional realm, they have the final word and it is infallible.

In spite of the fact that traditional leaders are the key persons of the Baatonu society, few younger missionaries show interest in getting to know them and thus establishing an amiable relationship with them. This work attempts to highlight the lack of understanding and the prejudices on both sides. Aiming to insist on the need for a convivial relationship between traditional leaders and missionaries, the article promotes and encourages dialogue and collaboration.

Introduction

The paper considers the terrain of conviviality and dialogue between traditional leaders and missionaries among the Baatombu. The titles traditional chiefs, traditional leaders, native leaders and crowned heads refer to one and the same Baatonu governing body in cultural and traditional aspects of life. As SMA missionaries, we know the status and characteristics of missionaries. This is not the case for all readers when it comes to Baatonu traditional leaders. So, before we get into the subject, here is a brief introduction to the Baatonu people and the organisation of their society.

Part One

Reaching out to a group in the Baatonu society: The traditional leaders

Geographical and demographic descriptions

The Baatombu live mainly in the department of Borgou and Alibori, located in the north-east of Benin and the north-west of Nigeria. The population of the Republic of Benin is 12, 864, 634; in which the population of Borgou-Alibori is 1, 245, 264. The principal occupations in these two regions are agriculture, animal rearing and hunting. The official languages are Baatonum, Boo, Fulfulde, Dendi, Ditammari and Nago.

Origin of the Baatonu people and their socio-political organisation

At the arrival of the Wassangari, warriors and adventurers, an ethnic group of Bussa settled in Ouénou towards the end of the 15th century. Before that, Borgou, the Baatonu region, was occupied by Voltaic-speaking populations - the Natimba, the Yoabu, the Pila-Pila, the Tienga, the Gourmantché, and then by Yoruba hunters, the Mokollé and the Baatombu. The Wassangari mix with the Baatombu and yet do not share their authority which allows them to form a ruling class of princes and kings to govern the Baatonu population. Over time they adopted the local language and certain local customs. They married Baatonu women. Through cohabitation and intermingling, there exists a close and convivial relationship between the Baatombu and the Wassangari, aristocratic horsemen. As a result, in Nikki kingdom, the Baatombu occupy titles and functions such as native leaders (sina dumwiru) and members of the council of ministers of Nikki kingdom. The Wassangari and the Baatombu live in harmony and govern Borgou and Alibori socio-culturally. The capital of the kingdom is the town of Nikki.

The Nikki kingdom is composed of four major groups: 1) the Wassangari, 2) the Baatombu, 3) the Gando, 4) and the foreigners. Though endogamous marriage is practiced among the Baatombu, exogamy is tolerated except in the case of marriage with the Gandos.

Regardless of democratic governance, the Baatombu abide by the precepts of the king (sina boko) in matters of traditional, socio-cultural and religious concerns. The role of the king is to personify the supreme authority to govern and to protect the people, to manage the affairs of the kingdom and to maintain unity and peace.

Traditional leaders

The Sina boko of Nikki governs each Baatonu village of the Borgou – Alibori regions in collaboration with a crowned prince. The prince represents among his people His Majesty the King of Nikki. With his blessing and accord, the local king gathers his council to ensure protection, unity and peace.

In his book, Benjamin Lee Hegeman, an American evangelical researcher and pastor, mentions numerous attacks and defeats that the Nikki kingdom has faced since the 15th century. The reasons behind its restless past are mainly religious wars, colonial, political and economic interests. According to Hegeman, the Nikki kingdom suffered humiliation because of successive defeats. He pinpoints seven historical events[1] that left deep wounds in the memory of the royal court and of the Baatonu people.

Today, as we pass through towns and villages, the royal courts almost look like ruined palaces. Some kings complain about their low revenue. Two-thirds of the population does not pay their contribution for the subsistence of the local king. There is also a decline of respect towards the king. For instance, in the past, to greet the local king in his palace or on the street, one had to take off his shoes and fall prostrate before the king whereas nowadays, one hardly bows his head. Here is an anecdote: the king of Pèrèrè collects grass in the Catholic mission campus for feeding his horse. When he finishes collecting the grass, he then requests the help of some local men to bring the grass bundles to his palace. Jokingly, the king says that he was quite content in his palace.

---

[1] Seven historical events that caused shame for the Baatombu are as follows : the trade tragedy, the establishment of a french and british military base, the final defeat of the Wassangari army in 1897, the World War, the arrival of white missionaries, the construction of roads by forced labour, the establishment of foreign schools, the imposition of hundreds of foreign governement rules and the posting of Dahomean middle men and civil servants in the baatonu territory, the Marxist-Leninist revolution (1974 – 1988) and liberal globalisation following the free and democratic elections of 1990, have weakened socio-political and traditional sovereignity at many levels. B. L. Hegeman, *l'Evangile en pays baatonu (Benin)*, Paris 2018, 29-34.

But since he was given a horse, he has to gather grass for it. Normally, the village youth should be at his service but they don't come forward. The worst thing is that the king carries the grass bundles on his head that has been crowned.

The scenario changes on Friday morning, the day scheduled to pay tribute to the local king. The local drums are played at the entrance of the palace. In the royal courtyard of Nikki the sacred drums and the local musicians play traditional drums in the courtyard. Fridays are reserved solely for paying homage to the king and in return receiving the king's blessing. During the week, the king is available for audience. Every year in the month of Gaani[2] the Baatombu gather around the sovereign king to celebrate the New Year. During this festival, the king of Nikki and his ministers go out of the royal palace to visit the territory, to invoke the ancestors and protective spirits and to bless the inhabitants of the kingdom.

Preconceived ideas from two sides

There is a Baatonu proverb whose literal translation goes like this, "The foreigner has big eyes but cannot see." The meaning of the proverb is that the foreigner does not know many things that the native people know. The outsiders think that the villagers know nothing. Both of them underestimate one another. First of all, I present here the missionaries' preconceptions and prejudices about traditional leaders that I gathered during informal sharing with some young missionaries.

Due to the historical events that shook the Baatonu society, the influence of the traditional chiefs does not have the same weight as before. Consequently, the missionaries feel that the glory of the Nikki kingdom is empty. Similarly, when a missionary first arrives on his mission field, he is eager to visit the king. Gradually, such interest fades away as there is nothing extraordinary. While visiting the palace, one observes cobwebs and how badly maintained the place is. At the sight of these, some missionaries develop an attitude of disrespect towards the kingdom.

Moreover, according to the general impression of foreigners, the royal court is demanding. Before being allowed to go to the palace, one is required to take off one's shoes and wait for a long time; when arriving in front of the king's throne, one has to prostrate oneself or genuflect.

---

[2] Gaani is one of the cultural festivals among the Baatombu to celebrate the new year.

After all, the king utters nothing important but only words of thanks for the visit and words of blessing. The visit does not stimulate further curiosity or desire to visit the palace again. Furthermore, prostrating before the king raises many religious questions: why to prostrate in front of a mortal body as if he were a god?

As the majority of the royal court dignitaries are Muslims, the common fear is that they do not like other religions. If so, why mingle with them and get into trouble? It would be better to keep a distance. Indeed, the bitter experiences of the pioneer missionaries provoke fear of being poisoned and witchcraft and death. It inhibits the contemporary missionaries from getting close to the traditional leaders.

When a missionary arrives in a country, he obtains administrative papers. The possession of papers like a visa, a work permit or resident permit makes him believe that he has the absolute right to reside, to incorporate into the society and to take part actively. He has fulfilled the administrative requirements, but he ignores the social requirement which is to make contact with local traditional leaders.

As for some missionaries, they are at the service of a vast mission territory or they are busy with many concerns such as the construction of the parish church, chapels, bore wells, boarding schools, dispensaries, alphabetisation programmes or any rural development projects. Some of them desire convivial relationship with the traditional leaders but they have no time.

So far, we have briefly touched on the preconceptions of missionaries. In the upcoming section we explore how traditional leaders perceive missionaries. Here I present a synthesis of responses that I collected from three traditional leaders, namely the prime minister of Nikki, the king of Pèrèrè and the king of Tontaru. According to them, the Baatombu are known for their hospitality. Nowadays, because of deceit, trickery and robbery, many people are reluctant to receive foreigners. Everyone, including foreigners, civil servants and missionaries are all welcome to the Baatonu territory. They come to serve the locality, to help and to improve the living conditions at various levels. There is no reason to reject or oppose them when they come to work for the benefit of the population.

On the other hand, the traditional authorities keep a critical eye on a stranger or institution that integrates into any Baatonu territory for the traditional leaders are concerned about the unity and peace amidst the population. The cold attitude or suspicious look at a stranger does not mean a rejection or opposition but rather, a scrutiny to discern the credibility of the stranger.

With regard to resistance to Christianity and its followers, the prime minister of Nikki refutes this opinion affirming: "Though the Nikki kingdom members are predominantly Muslims, the traditional leaders welcome believers of other religions. For example, among the local kings, there are Christian and animist kings. The kingdom has two principles with regard to religions: firstly, the members of the kingdom follow the footsteps of their ancestors. If someone wants to worship other gods, the court does not have any objection. Secondly, every religion works to promote peace and unity which is the primary concern of the traditional leaders as well. So there is no reason to set obstacles before any religion that works for the same cause.

A traditional chief expresses his unhappiness when a stranger ignores the traditional authorities. It is noticed that he is close to civil servants, doctors, nurses, the police commissioner, the village delegate, but he has no consideration for the local king and his council. Are they not also at the service of the population? It is still worse when some missionaries behave like this. They, who learn the language and culture well, aren't they supposed to know the customs and show minimum courtesy towards the local leaders? The missionaries work closely with the Baatonu people who are the property of the Baatonu land. They have their own cultural and traditional leaders. At this juncture, the Pèrèrè king makes a comparison saying, "Before entering into a legitimate relationship with a girl, the young man must manifest respect towards her parents. Otherwise, they tend to conclude that he is not well educated. If he ignores her parents, it means that he considers the girl a prostitute or an orphan. Isn't it so? Similarly, before working closely with people, it is better that the local leaders are rendered due respect and consideration".

The Nikki prime minister reveals a spiritual outlook among the Baatombu explaining, "The Baatonu territory is under the possession of spiritual proprietors. They are none other than protector – spirits and the ancestors who had inhabited in the land. They continue to be the owners and protectors of the place. When someone intends to stay in that place, the ancestors and their spirit-protectors have to be invoked. For this reason, it is important that an individual or an institution, that plans to install something new, should present the project to the local traditional leader who, in turn, invokes the spirits and ancestors to ensure a pleasant and fruitful stay. Without the blessing no enterprise will bear fruit."

Social implications of these ideas

On the one hand, mission work undertaken without consideration of traditional and social systems is fruitless because it has no social or cultural roots. On the other hand, if missionaries want to take into consideration all the customs and beliefs of the environment, the pursuit of missionary work will be impossible. For this reason, some missionaries deliberately ignore the local authorities so that missionary tasks can be carried out with efficiency and innovation. One may find many more valid and concrete reasons which support this point of view. However, in my opinion, convivial relationships with traditional leaders are an advantage for the mission. We will explore the reasons later. Before that, the second part of the article enumerates the initiatives that are undertaken in order to build a good relationship with the traditional leaders.

Part Two

Building bridges

The initiatives being tried out in the mission field are solely the result of spontaneity and intuition. I have learnt some of these initiatives from senior missionaries and from diocesan priests in the mission field.

We visit the local king's palace to greet him or to introduce a missionary or a seminarian or a visitor who has newly arrived.

On other occasions, we consult the king for some information or explanation regarding a socio-cultural or traditional aspect of life. In general, the king is impressed by the missionary's interest in deepening his understanding of Baatonu culture. So, he explains and he invites the members of his council to verify and add to his point of view.

From time to time, I give a brief account of my activities, my pursuits, my findings and my expectations. The three traditional chiefs that I have known listen to me keenly and attentively. The Baatonu prime minister welcomes me with joy always. When the mission faces some difficult situations, I consult him and he gives me the historical or socio-cultural keys to understand the event or the Baatonu spirit better. In fact, he does not change or oppose any mission project but rather, shows the right way (Baatonu way) of doing it.

At parish celebrations or important events in the parish, the parish council invites the local traditional leader. During the feast, he is invited to address the assembly. In his message, he pronounces blessings, words of encouragement and thanks.

In return, the king invites the priests and the faithful to important events in his palace. We regularly take part in the festivity of the royal court.

Responses from concerned persons

The response to these initiatives has been positive. Through frequent visits, we get accustomed to the palace and audience with the king is obtained easily. Even if the visit to the king is time consuming and one could be doing other useful things, it is still worth it for the sake of establishing space for conviviality and dialogue because it edifies both parties. I quote the wise words of an experienced missionary who says, "The quality of a dynamic missionary is not solely about doing but rather in the way of being."

The traditional leaders are happy when they are considered and invited to take part in the important events of the mission. In their address, they encourage the faithful to unity and sincere collaboration with the missionaries for a better world. Through good understanding, they intervene promptly to solve a problem and restore peace. The traditional leaders exhort the population to work hard in the Church to safeguard peace and unity.

Response from the outside world

The population manifests joy deriving from the conviviality between its traditional leaders and the Church. Similarly, at the diocesan level, the bishop encourages his clergy, his pastoral collaborators and the Church to promote and maintain conviviality and dialogue. Recognizing their traditional wisdom, the diocesan commission for interreligious and intercultural dialogue invites them to help deepen cultural or social knowledge on various themes.

This attempt is inspired by the spirit of the Second Vatican Council, which teaches the local Church in these terms: "All men are called to belong to the people of God. The Church or People of God, in establishing that kingdom takes nothing away from the temporal welfare of any people; on the contrary, it fosters and takes to itself, insofar as they are good, the ability, riches and customs in which the genius of each people expresses itself. Taking them to itself, it purifies, strengthens, elevates and ennobles them. In virtue of this catholicity, each individual part contributes through its special gifts to the food of the other parts and of the whole church, through the common sharing of gifts and through the common effort to attain fullness in unity." The broad mindedness of the Council encourages every Christian to reach out to all people, all cultures and why not to traditional leaders.

Part Three

General reflection from experience

This part has three sections: 1) conviviality from the personal point of view, 2) need for conviviality in the mission of the Church today and 3) in the SMA mission.

From my point of view, initiatives in favour of conviviality and dialogue are necessary. When we look back at the history of evangelisation in Benin, incidences of suspicion, poisoning, attempted murder, expulsion of missionaries were prevalent and frequent. Yet, many missionaries, and in particular three French missionaries, Fathers François Steinmetz, Louis Parisot and Francis Aupiais, were able to gain the confidence of the traditional chiefs. At the initial stage of my ministry here, people treated me with suspicion and mistrust. Gradually, relationships matured. I here acknowledge also the good guidance of senior missionaries. They passed on their knowledge of the local culture and language which helped me to have an open mind and to appreciate the Baatonu people.

In fact, conviviality resulted in timely help in my pastoral work. Here I give an account of two incidents where the traditional leaders were of great support. Firstly, when a Catholic woman was attacked and was about to be beaten to death because she was suspected to be a witch, the Baatonu prime minister came to her rescue. This woman was involved in the Church and was running a small shop in a village. Her commercial success provoked jealousy in the village. One day, some village youths rose up against her to beat her to death, expel her family members from the village and set fire to her house. The police intervened and rescued them all. When the youths learned that the family had taken refuge in the parish, they threatened to attack the presbytery. The anger of these villagers was furious and unquenched. They wanted to kill the so- called witch at all costs. How could peace be restored in the village? How could the woman and her family get reintegrated into the community? In this critical situation the Baatonu prime minister was able to resolve the problem through his personal intervention.

Another incident took place in a remote village community where the majority of the population is Muslim. A member of the Catholic community, under the so-called impulse of the spirit, declared someone a witch. This kindled a frenzied attack on the community. The Muslims in the village took the chance to expel the Christians and to destroy the chapel. On this occasion, the traditional leaders supported the Catholics.

At this juncture, we take a moment to examine the secret of the traditional authority. In an interview, the Nikki prime minister revealed the secret: the reason why people abide by the final decision of the traditional leaders is due to the blessing or the curse pronounced by the voice of their traditional chiefs. Indeed, every man should seek blessings and avoid curses. Success in life, mental and physical health, prosperity and fruitfulness are fruits of blessings that one possesses. On the contrary, when a person brings a curse on himself, the negative impact of the curse affects his family and even his descendants. Consequently, all bad things such as illness, sterility, bad luck, famine and even death will invade the family. He added that the Baatombu would dare to take up arms but would fear curses. A curse is the most deadly weapon in the world.

For the mission of the Church today

Before dealing with mission initiatives of the Church today, it is useful to review briefly the history of the evangelisation of Benin. In the 15th century, Portuguese ships were exploring the coast of Guinea. On one hand, they were in search of wealth for the king, and on the other, the royal maritime charter required the promotion of Christianity as a political strategy to confront Islam, which was the greatest commercial and religious rival. These explorations opened up new possibilities for Catholic missionaries in the Bay of Benin. At that time, the missionaries aimed at the conversion of the king as they thought that his conversion would lead to the conversion of the whole nation. The strategy was successful and many African kings became Catholics in order to get political and economic benefits. For example, a Yoruba king from the kingdom of Oyo Benin requested Portugal to send Christian soldiers and holy teachers. But as he had not yet been baptised, his request was not granted until his baptism. He was finally deemed fit to receive military aid. Unfortunately, the churches founded as a result of king's baptism disappeared very shortly afterwards. Another strategy was to build

Catholic chapels, dispensaries and schools with boarding facilities. Evangelisation took the form of humanitarian works. Nowadays, the Church's mission does not need to hide its identity because there are no political or economic interests or benefits. It must reach out to everyone in a fraternal and open spirit, making room for conviviality, dialogue and collaboration.

For the SMA mission

As mentioned earlier, the Baatonu society has a history wounded by turmoil and humiliating incidents. Consequently, the Baatonu people have a suspicious attitude towards anything that is foreign to them. The Church had a difficult beginning due to that. The missionaries had to endure many difficulties in announcing the Gospel. Let us glance at Borghero's missionary approach. When he arrived in Ouidah, he asked for an audience with king Glélé because he realised that, without the king's goodwill, he would not be able to carry out the mission and perhaps he would not even be allowed to stay there. So, during his visit, he wanted to explain to the king about his missionary status and his mission. The king, however, was convinced that Borghero was an ambassador from Europe coming to pay tribute to the king of Dahomey and also to pursue the slave trade. Eventually, he was given accommodation by the servants who supervised his activities. He could not leave Ouidah and was not allowed to evangelize. In view of this he decided to meet the king again and the audience was granted. Borghero clarified the purpose of his presence in Benin, his state of priesthood and celibacy. He also courageously stated his disagreement concerning the immolation of human victims and the slave trade. The evangelisation of the kingdom of Dahomey sounded important, strategic and urgent to him, but the hour had not yet come. He consoled himself reasoning as follows: "God does not need to go quickly. St. Benedict in the sixth century of the Church still found idols to break, pagans to convert, and that at the very gates of Rome. Let us not assume that we can move faster than the great apostles. God alone knows His purposes, but judging as we can, I would say to you that this people seem fit for the kingdom of God."

That is the missionary secret: patience, perseverance and enthusiasm in missionary commitment and in all human relationships. In the Baatonu region, the traditional leaders testify to the numerous and tireless efforts of the missionaries, for example, the missionary quality of Father Ferdinand Bioret and others. The good relationship that the senior missionaries left behind is a model for contemporary missionaries. Following that example, today's missionaries are duty bound to safeguard and promote the convivial relationship with traditional leaders.

Conclusion

In the SMA missionary tradition, visiting and collaborating with traditional authorities was a classic and fundamental step before starting any missionary work. Whether traditional leaders supported the mission or not, was not the primary concern of this article. Instead, the key point is to understand that traditional leaders are the custodians of the local culture. They are the ones who coordinate govern and guide daily life in Baatonu country. In order to be well accepted a missionary must be acquainted with the key people of the society. Traditional leaders can train missionaries to understand the Baatonu way of being and doing. Such exercise may seem hard or even ridiculous or a waste of time. But it is worth learning from them. Otherwise, a zealous and dynamic missionary approach, without respecting the local leaders, may seem an attempt to impose, dominate or provoke resulting in a clash of cultures and religions. Today, evangelisation is not any more an imposition, not a negotiation, nor a bargain born out of political and economic interests. It is born solely out of life witness that builds upon human relationships and fraternity, making room for dialogue and collaboration to achieve that better world that Jesus dreamt of.

Bibliography

HEGEMAN, B. L., *L'Evangile en pays baatonou (Benin)*, Paris 2018.

GANTLY, P., Mission to West Africa I, ADM 2006.

Marchand, P., *Baaton Monnu, Proverbes en Bariba*, Parakou 1988.

BIGOU, L. B. B., *Elements d'anthropologie et d'histoire du Nord-Bénin*, Cotonou 1994.

SECOND VATICAN COUNCIL, *Lumen Gentium*, Rome 1964.

Mission to the victims of violence

Richard Angolio SMA

Systemic violence, in the way that we SMA have experienced it in northern Nigeria and in East Africa, is no longer an occasional occurrence, on the peripheries of the African reality today. It is often at the centre of the ministry that we are called to engage in by Jesus, and by our charism.

The testimonies that we hear from all sides are challenging. They are at times difficult to listen to and to take in. Even more so is our own experience of violence on the ground! On one level, we are faced with practical questions—what should we say? What can we possibly do? How can I be present? Where can I find the inner strength to work with victims of systemic violence? What changes, in the long run, will exposure to these high-stress situations bring about in me? On a more abstract level, we are left wondering what can explain the willingness of human beings to indiscriminately target other ethnic groups. From our experience in counselling we know that violence takes a toll on the perpetrator as well as on the victim. Because of what we have seen we are left wondering whether the perpetrators have left their humanity behind them. What happened?

This article is an attempt to come to terms with the violence we see, with our own shortcomings, and with the changes that these situations bring about in us.

My own experience in Nigeria

Here is an illustration that might remind you of pastoral experience you may have had. It was night, and I was asleep. Around 3 a.m., my cell phone rang. The caller was a parishioner. Given the timing, I was ready for bad news, and I was right. The message was straightforward: "We have been attacked in our village and seven men are dead, it is terrible!" Silence! Then he went on, "Am calling just to let you know, I know you cannot come now. If God permits us, we shall see each other in the morning." A small exchange of words and then we ended with our usual night goodbye: "May God bring us to the morning."

As you can imagine, I couldn't sleep after that, and at dawn we were all gathered in the village where the killings had taken place. On entering the village, I met children, some only five years old. They were carrying small stones in their hands and I understood why. They were ready to defend themselves. But what could these little hands and stones do? I wondered where they had been all that night. I felt as desperate as those little children. Usually, I can keep myself from crying at the sight of wounds from machetes and gun shots. I can hold back my tears, even upon seeing corpses covered in blood lying on the hard ground, but that moment was different. I cried.

Later I came to learn that even babies had been injured in the course of that horrific attack. It looked as if everything had blood on it. I saw a mattress soaked in blood on the cement floor. I was unable to absorb all the images of the spilled blood. I heard the cries of women and saw desperation in every eye. On trying to walk, my steps became feeble and my throat suddenly became hoarse.

There was nothing I could say, or even think of saying. Many images were flashing in my mind: the weddings and baptisms we had celebrated amid great jubilation, the wonderful songs and dances we had enjoyed a week earlier (some of our best singers and dancers were victims), the plans we had made for the future, and much more.

Unable to know what would come next, a brother to one of those massacred led me to other venues where the attack had taken place and showed me some of the visible traces. I heard one lady say in tears, "And all we are told is to forgive." Thank God, something stopped me from uttering any kind of pious platitude. I was in shock, and time stood still. In my long silence, I was surprised when someone else spoke to me saying, "Take heart."

With the "Take heart", the realisation came to me that we were all caught up in this horrific experience together. We were all hurting. The truth is that I didn't have to search for consoling words. My presence was enough, and it said it all. I just hoped that what I felt was true, that just as I felt consoled with those words, the traumatised crowd was also consoled by my silent presence.

The irony is that it was someone who felt an even deeper pain than I did who consoled me. To spare you from the traumatizing events that followed, suffice to say that this situation awakened in me a new understanding; namely, there will always be something to share even when all we are left with is our awareness and our willingness to share.

The larger picture

My experience is not unique. Terrorism of all stripes and colours has emerged as a world-wide phenomenon. It stands in direct opposition to Gospel values. Specifically, the persecution of Christians is rapidly becoming ubiquitous in our time. Recently, in the Nigerian context, we have heard of 21 killed, 26 killed, 52 killed, and it never ends.

There was an occasion in northern Nigeria, when 202 people were killed, and their houses burned. Farms and grain supplies were also targeted. These are not just numbers but individual people, each with a story and a dream. They are people we have lived with, worked with, and loved. Of course, you won't get it on the international news. If you did, you wouldn't get any details, telling you how blood was poured downstream by the killers with the accompanying words, "Let them drink their own people's blood."

After yet another occurrence, I met a widow who had lost five sons. She asked me how she was supposed to go on trusting and praying. With a big sigh, she said, "I am tired!" When these things happen, those living who remain behind are left to mourn, to imagine a way forward and to keep on living. But how? One is always waiting for the other shoe to drop, for violence to erupt again.

Unless we ask crucial and meaningful questions

Who are the killers, and why do they kill? The answer from the political analysts is that they are Boko Haram and/or Fulani herdsmen. This could very well be true; however, I feel that labelling them is really pushing them to one side, transforming them into a cipher, and leaving unasked questions about who they are as human beings. While this labelling may serve the needs of socio-political analysts, it does not begin to address the concerns of bearers of the Gospel. Yet it must be said that killing in God's name reveals that something is wrong with our image of God and of who we are as His creatures. Whichever side of the divide we choose to take, all our differences are intertwined in humanity.[1]

A consideration of ingratitude

What can we say about ourselves and our own relationship with a humanizing God? In Northern Nigeria, there is a certain type of bean that is rarely eaten, even though these beans are readily available. They have a peculiar name, *achi chiru*, literally translated from the Hausa language as, *"to be eaten in silence."*

One would wonder why we should be encouraged to eat in silence, when sharing a meal is a social event that is usually accompanied by the sharing of pleasantries and humorous stories. … Well, there is a reason for this: for those who gave these beans the name, silence stops one from complaining about the lack of something better to eat, especially when s/he lacks the good sense to be grateful for having a meal to begin with. Silence stops one from being ungrateful for what may seem to be a poor meal when others may thank the heavens unceasingly if they got even same food. The danger of our unmet expectations is that we end up complaining, and thus become blind to what we ought to be grateful for. We end up sinning against the providence that God has given us

Now, let's be honest! There may be, in fact, times when we have complained. In the past, we have thought some things to be of great value, until the moment we were confronted with the realities of the lives of other people in dire need, in great helplessness, or in obvious powerlessness. Only then do we realize that we shouldn't have complained in the first place. The fact of the matter is that we could just as well have done without that which we thought indispensable. Jesus reminds us that "…the poor you will always have with you" (Mt 26: 11), — Why? One reason is to inspire us to focus on the gifts we have received and to remember that there is always someone else less fortunate than us.

---

[1] An African proverb says, cut one finger and the rest are covered in blood. We cannot successfully hurt a fellow human being without hurting ourselves. The silence of relevant opinion makers on such a crucial matter is concerning and if it does not disturb us, then what else will?

As noted above, the irony is that when hardship pushes people to their lowest ebb, we do not hear them complaining; in fact, we are often surprised at their endurance and resilience, and we sometimes wonder what their source of strength might be, in the face of how rough their life has been.

As an aside, perhaps they do not complain because they have learned the hard truth that their opinions do not matter in this world of ours. Their cry is like the cry of fish in the water. Who could tell the difference? I remember the time that a man who wanted to tell me why he was contented in life jokingly said, "Why complain when half the people won't listen to you and the rest don't care anyway?" If we bother to complain, we end up getting frustrated and wonder why we bothered. We lose the peace we have been searching for. Indeed it is rewarding to be grateful and stop at that. Furthermore, when our hearts have the least spark of gratitude, they are ready to share the gift of life and its riches, among them faith. Genuine sharing of faith is born of gratitude.

Let us pause here to say that faith has eyes that see the invisible, and those of us who possess faith must never cease making sure that the voiceless have the opportunity to make themselves heard by the wider society. It is this kind of meaningful praxis that brings liberation.

Sharing our resources and sharing the Gospel

There is a link between our sense of gratitude and our readiness to share. We are given a template for our behaviour again and again in the Scriptures; the Torah is very clear about our responsibility to share our resources: "If among you, one of your brothers should become poor, in any of your towns within your land that the Lord your God is giving you, you shall not harden your heart or shut your hand against your poor brother, but you shall open your hand to him and lend him sufficient for his need, whatever it may be ..." (Deut. 15: 7-11). When we abide by these words, we are imitating God who is the giver *par excellence*.

The New Testament echoes this idea: all we are and have has been given us from heaven (Jn 3: 27). Here we must accept that the first and the greatest gift is our life. St. Paul, on his part, encourages us to give thanks to God for all we have received (1 Th 5: 18), and in humility to be concerned for the well-being of others (Phil. 2: 3-4).

The Gospels themselves make this idea abundantly clear. The parable of the ten lepers (Lk 17: 11-19) not only teaches us to be grateful for all that we are and have received; it also reveals to us the basic difference between God and human beings. God doesn't wait for a thank you. It expresses the difference between the way God gives and the way we give--God's sharing and our sharing.

When mothers, and indeed all of us, are training children in good manners and life skills, such as appreciating the gifts and sacrifices of others, we remind them, "And what do you say?" As soon as the child says thank you, we congratulate them — we reinforce in them the link between the words "thank you" and receiving a gift. Cynically one might observe that in the end, once conditioned, they will always say thank you in order to secure tomorrow's gift.

In the parable of the ten lepers, Jesus, who is aware of the ingratitude of the 'other nine' lepers, gives them the gift of healing anyway. Jesus gave the same gift to all, the one with gratitude and the others without, Jews and the Samaritan alike. God's generosity overlooks our ingratitude. Our basic stance of Christian gratitude can bring us closer to the source of all goodness. And in the long run, we are the ultimate beneficiaries of our gratitude.

Learning to share as Christ did

To return to the single leper who came back to give thanks and to glorify God, Jesus said, "Rise and go, your faith has saved you" (Lk 17: 19). Our gratitude is a way of acknowledging and expressing our faith in God. The Samaritan leper's gratitude was accompanied by a gesture of throwing himself at the feet of Jesus. This is a gesture of worship and a form of prayer, a prayer that brought him even a greater gift; namely, salvation.

Let us return to our focus of this reflection — the victims of systemic violence. We share what we have and even sometimes what we do not have. That we can share what we have is easy to fathom, but when the sense of our common humanity summons us to share, it dares us to share even that which we do not have. It may even ask us to share despite our inability to see in ourselves anything worth sharing. We may feel a lack of confidence in the possibility of a further sharing process.

When it comes to sharing in the pains and struggles of others, sharing from our emptiness does not come easily. Notwithstanding, in our weakness and our feeling of inadequacy, in our feeling of emptiness, we can still share. To paraphrase St. John Paul II, even the poor have something to give. Jesus praises the sharing of the destitute, for it spares nothing, as best exemplified by the widow's mite (Lk 21: 1-4). This is a giving in which one surrenders to divine providence rather than relying on oneself or other people.

When that which is to be given is something intangible, such as words, this kind of giving demands the gift of our presence, even if it be a silent presence. Yes, sometimes suitable words can vanish from our minds in a moment. There comes a time when we cannot find the right words to comfort a friend or a relative who is hurting. If we do find some, they may be very good words and well-intentioned, but they may turn out to not be what is needed at that particular moment. Instead of soothing, they may only reignite the pangs of pain in the one we wish to console. For this reason, the Swahili speakers say, *ajikwaaye haambiwi pole*, in English, *do not say sorry to one who stumbles*. The deeper meaning of this is that when one is struggling to get somewhere, words of sympathy may make that person despair.

In the words of Pope Francis: "There are Christians whose lives are like Lent without Easter. ... People who have to endure great suffering." These are the people in whose life experiences we are called to share as a way of ministering to them. These are "the most abandoned" of whom Venerable Melchior de Marion Brésillac speaks. Pointing to our necessary response, Pope Francis continues: "...yet slowly but surely we all have to let the joy of faith slowly revive as a quiet yet firm trust, even amid the greatest distress" (*Evangelii Gaudium* no. 6).

So, when Jesus commands his disciples: "Freely you have received, freely give" (Mt 10: 8), this includes sharing what we do not know, what we are yet to learn. We do not come as experts in matters of faith or as some genius who has learnt it all. We come as students of Christ the teacher, always students. Together with all those who seek the knowledge of God, we approach the presence of God in each other, in our bare feet like Moses at the burning bush (Ex 3: 5). We should be always ready to learn and share what we have already mastered.

Humanity grows richer when we share the unique truths we have learnt and experienced about God in our diversity. Our challenge to keep sharing does not stop with terror and persecutions.

It goes without saying that where there are persecutions, there too are many other forms of human sufferings. In our ministry, we have to deal with many other social issues, including the increasing unemployment of youth— a reality that engenders hopelessness and the numerous repercussions that come with it. Sometimes unemployment is due to non-functioning or corrupt governments, and only faith-based interventions may inspire hope for the underprivileged people amid widespread, abject poverty.

Sometimes we have to deal with an over-burdened health care system, with lack of relevant social amenities, with issues related to immigration and urbanisation, with failing education and justice systems, and with a blindness to the degradation of the environment. There's no way I can detail all the problems we face in our outreach.

I want to focus on this last issue for a moment—that of the environment. I think that this is one issue in the African reality that does not concern us enough. As we know, in the view of St. Paul, it is the whole creation that has been groaning in the pains of childbirth, right up to the present time, awaiting redemption (Rm 8: 22). I mention it here, because there is, in fact, no quick solution to the impasse that faces us. Our response as Christians, and particularly as Catholics, should be arrived at through the lens of the gospel.

All in all, the demands of the Gospel remain constant: we are called to share the gift of life and to encourage this sharing. We strive to remain faithful in our willingness to share. As part of our response, we need to teach important life skills necessary for the continuation of life on this planet and future generations. These may include communication, teamwork, flexibility, critical thinking, and mindfulness of who we are called to be, to mention but a few. We do this knowing that sharing our resources is the bedrock of justice and peace.

The Gospel is always demanding because, "whenever our interior life becomes caught up in its own interests and concerns, there is no longer room for others, no place for the poor. God's voice is no longer heard, the quiet joy of his love is no longer felt, and the desire to do good fades" (*Evangelii Gaudium* no. 2).

Dealing with anxiety

Despite our efforts to meet human challenges and alleviate suffering, there are ever increasing cries for help. We meet them in our missionary outreach every day. Working under these conditions can build up pressure within us and take away our joy, and our peace, and render us anxious. This happens especially in moments when we feel as empty and as helpless as those we are called to minister to.

Researchers working in the field of the behavioural sciences teach us that "anxiety and tensions are essential functions of living, just as hunger and thirst are. They are our self-protective reactions when we are confronted by threats to our safety, well-being, happiness or self-esteem" (Stevenson 1962, pp. 384-385). In spite of their being part of life's defence system, we should be aware of the harm they can cause. The same researchers warn us to be "watchful when our emotional upsets become more frequent and when they shake us severely." When anxiety becomes chronic it can be detrimental to our health and to our Christian vocation. Some people speak of burnout —physical or mental collapse, usually caused by overworking, stress or unfruitful work.

Concerned teachers, medical practitioners, business people and many different types of workers know this. As individuals and in groups, they seek remedies in the solutions provided by modern science: scheduling your recreation; taking one thing at a time; shunning the superman urge; going easy with criticism; talking it out with someone.[2] As people of faith and ministers of the Gospel, we accept and use these recommendations too; for example, we talk to a friend who is human like us, one we trust will listen to us and help us, but more importantly, we talk to Jesus, who also calls us friends (Jn 15: 15).

Parting words

It is while sharing and conversing with our Divine Friend in prayer that we may find relevant the following text from Archbishop Oscar Romero.

It helps, now and then, to step back and take a long view. The kingdom is not only beyond our efforts, it is even beyond our vision. We accomplish in our lifetime only a tiny fraction of the magnificent enterprise that is God's work. Nothing we do is complete, which is a way of saying that the kingdom always lies beyond us.

No statement says all that could be said.
No prayer fully expresses our faith.
No confession brings perfection.
No pastoral visit brings wholeness.
No program accomplishes the Church's mission.
No set of goals and objectives includes everything.
This is what we are about.
We plant the seeds that one day will grow.
We water seeds that are already planted, knowing that they hold
    future promise.
We lay foundations that will need further development.

---

[2] *Ibid.*, 384.

We provide yeast that expands far beyond our capabilities.

We cannot do everything, and there is a sense of liberation in realizing that.

This enables us to do something, and to do it very well.

It may be incomplete, but it is a beginning, a step along the way, an opportunity for the Lord's grace to enter and to do the rest.

We may never see the end results, but that is the difference between the master builder and the worker.

We are workers, not master builders; ministers, not messiahs.

We are prophets of a future not our own.

The Renaissance artist Leonardo da Vinci was right in saying, "A work of art is never completed; it is only abandoned." Abandoned, in the sense that it is left open to be continued. We are co-workers in God's great project, a project greater than us. We are here to do our part, our best. It is God who brings this work to its good end.

Bibliography

AKINOLA, « History: Usman Dan Fodio Biography, Works and Wars, (The Legend). »

https ://www.tekemetonaija.com/2017/10/history-usman-dan-fodio-biography-wars.html, 2017: (Accessed on November 25th 2021).

BOLMAN, L. G., AND T. E. DEAL., Reframing Organizations. Artistry, Choice and Leadership, Danvers (MA) 2017[6].

MOSEBACH M., The 21, A journey into the Land of Coptic Martyrs, Translated by ALTA L. PRICE. New York 2020.

PAPE FRANÇOIS, Exhortation apostolique Evangelii Gaudium, Rome, 24 nov. 2013.

STEVENSON, S. G., « The Magical Ways to Inner Peace, How to Deal with Your Tensions », in Our Human Body, Its Wonders & Its Care, New York 1962.

Smell of the sheep: a missiological approach to evangelisation in Africa today

Charles Kouakou Adjoumani SMA

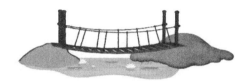

Africa is so rich in "culture" [1], but this cultural material has not been used adequately to improve human dignity or Christian identity faced with challenges. There is often a strong gap between Sunday worship and social life. One can be in church on Sunday morning when the liturgy is quite lively, if not "entertaining" and then participate without difficulty, in sacrifices to the ancestors and other practices contrary to the Christian faith, or a family or clan meeting where cultural norms determine everything. Other Africans may be simple Christian practitioners and not adhere to any cultural beliefs, but this also leaves them without roots in their Christianity. It is not that African culture is in direct

---

[1] The Pastoral Constitution on the Church in the Modern World *Gaudium et Spes* tells us that: "the word 'culture' in a broad sense refers to everything by which man refines and develops the many capacities of his mind and body; strives to subdue the universe through knowledge and work; humanizes social life, both family life and civil life as a whole, through the progress of morals and institutions; finally translates, communicates and preserves in his works, in the course of time, the great spiritual experiences and the major aspirations of man, so that they may serve the progress of many and even of the whole human race." (GS 53)

contradiction with the Christian values found in the liturgy or the teachings, but the cultural material of Africa is still today, very different from the current forms of Christianity. The mixing of the two cultures often results in the loss of a strong identity, whether as a Christian or as an African. This can lead to confusion if cultures are not listened to, and especially if personal encounters with the sacred or evil are not taken into account by pastoral agents.

The difference comes from the meaning and values of symbols and not so much from the fact that they are contradictory. Of course, depending on the choices and beliefs of the individual about these symbols, some people make the choice directly on those who speak to them the most, others associate them, and still others remain in confusion without anyone to guide them, especially in difficult times of life. The question is: how can a pastor know that one of the members of the flock is in this difficult confusion of values? Should the missionary care about those who struggle with these values?

The general objective of this article is to illustrate how missiology can respond to cultural identity to create a credible Christianity for Africans. To do so, let us identify some issues that so far require serious consideration, such as the large population of youth that represents about 60% of the African population. Secondly, we explore the model of evangelisation advocated by Pope Francis, especially his invitation to pastors to emanate the smell of their sheep or flock. Thirdly, the concept of initiation will serve as an example of a path to follow to bring the sheep back into the sheepfold, charitably and responsibly. We will conclude by presenting the implications of these suggestions.

Some demonstrations of how the sheep go astray these days

Africa is not immune to the current waves of globalisation that have been sweeping the world since the 1990s with the fall of the Berlin Wall in 1989. The globalisation we are going through these days is associated with liberal democracy but also with capitalism where everything is based on utilitarian motivations. The frantic race of people to meet basic human needs and to live with dignity leaves little room for reflection on the values of African culture or of Christianity. Unfortunately, many Christian communities are also affected by this utilitarian approach; and we hear things like: "As long as the few Christians participate in the life of the Church and the population increases, the Church is comfortable".

Is this not one of the causes of the proliferation of sects and their courage to propose themselves as an alternative to traditional churches?

Young people are often victims of these fanatical evangelisations because they are at the stage where they seek an identity for themselves. They need to be made aware that this is a problem. Without responding to the crisis they are going through, they are further misguided by turning to other sects that exploit them by preventing them from participating in the activities of their churches. Many could still be considered members of the Christian community, but this means nothing to them.

Catholics in Africa are most likely to lose one of their members to other denominations or to an African religion. The problem is not just about losing members to the mushrooming Pentecostal churches; the members are indeed lost in an endless search for the truth when certain situations of life occur. One wonders, why? The famous Anglican pastor John Mbiti, who belongs to the first generation of African theologians, has suggested a reason in these words: "At important moments in their lives, such as marriages, pregnancies, births, and baptisms, initiations and deaths, Africans are more likely to fall back on their culture than to follow Christianity." It may be said humorously: "to come to receive Holy Communion with the blood of the sacrifices on the hands during the day or on Sunday in the church, and go at night or during the week to the 'Fetishist'." However, questions remain regarding the missiological response to such trends. Are African pastors sensitive to this? What answers are given to Christians at such moments, especially in painful moments? Is there a missiological answer to this double consciousness? Why do people stop going to church? Is it not because they have not seen Christ as the true Fetishist, the healer, the one who forgives sins, the reconciler, the giver of life (John 10: 10), and especially as the Good Shepherd, patient and merciful towards them? It also takes into account the insensitivity of certain shepherds, priests, men and women religious, due to an exclusivist tendency, the ignorance and avoidance of African culture, thus avoiding any dialogue.

Mbiti's assertion remains a challenge but also a hope for African missionaries. It is a challenge that calls for a more committed response. Most nomadic shepherds know every sheep or livestock by name. Even children are raised to know that. It is thanks to the commitment to know and constantly count the sheep, so that they never lose them or just discover the absence of the sheep. Africans may not return to despair only at important moments in life, as Mbiti says but also and mainly during painful events.

Thus, in the present social reality of world challenges, evangelisation needs to go beyond cultures and reach the person. This goes back to the African philosophy of Ubuntu: «I am because we are and since we are, I am». The "us" part has often been emphasised in inculturation to the detriment of the "I", that is, the person in the community. If individuals do not conform to social values and norms, there could not be part of the "us". Also, the "I" can get lost in the identity of the "we"; hence the need for the shepherd to focus on individuals. While "we" is emphasised, in the African context, any "I" problem is also the "we" problem.

Pope Francis and the analogy of carrying the smell of sheep

The analogy of "the smell of sheep" is a powerful way to rethink the mission in Africa today. Pope Francis has always maintained that the shepherd of the People of God must be able to have the smell of the sheep himself. This has two implications: on the one hand, if the shepherd or shepherdess has the smell of the sheep, he or she will notice that some are missing. On the other hand, there is the involvement of the shepherd who emanates the smell of the sheep. In both cases, the need to protect the sheep is immanent. This is what we call pastoral care but also the new model of evangelisation. Ultimately, the goal is for the sheep to spread or seek the smell of the Good Shepherd: Christ himself. It is joy when the sheep have the mentality of the shepherd and can even go out through the door and return home safe and sound.

In *Evangelii Gaudium*, Pope Francis recalls that the Church must proclaim the Good News to the ends of the earth (Acts 1:8), but his methodology is radically different. The Holy Father describes "evangelisation as inculturation". The difference is that all evangelisation should be inculturation. Here inculturation applies to a universal scope, it applies to all cultures. There is indeed a subtle tendency of resistance to inculturation, coming from some who think that inculturation is something specific for Africa. Thus, to oppose this methodological approach of inculturation would be to hinder the action of the Holy Spirit. Why should missionaries in Africa be different? A similar view is shared by Virgilio Elizondo who gives an example of how the failure of evangelisation in Mexico has been transformed by a change in methodology. It was not easy, however, for Juan Diégo, to whom Our Lady of Guadalupe appeared, to go to the shepherd. Such shepherds - the bishops of that time, lived in palaces. He describes in poignant terms how Juan Diego had to convey the message to the bishop:

"After some difficulties, Juan Diego is instructed by the Lady to go to the top of the mountain where he will find the sign the bishop was asking for. When Juan Diego arrives at the top, he finds beautiful flowers from Castile in full bloom. He cuts them, puts them in his mantle (tilma), and takes them to the bishop. The missionaries had brought the gospel from Castile and now it was growing out of the heart of Mexican soil. As Juan Diego unfolded the tilma and the flowers were falling to the ground, the image of Our Lady of Guadalupe appeared on his tilma. The bishops knelt and asked for forgiveness. The image itself is a complex but harmonious pictorial message and together with the narrative presents the gospel of Jesus Christ in native terms. From this moment on, the people gradually started to regain their desire to live and to accept the gospel through their own symbols, rites, and rituals. Life now had meaning, and life was to be celebrated."[2]

In Africa, life does not often seem to make sense during violent conflict, corruption, and tribalism. The evangelising process has been improved, but there is still much to be done to improve it by investing in inculturation, by listening to people. The mission must be stripped of "fanaticism and put on an authentic evangelising fervour" (cf. EG 117).

Laurenti Magesa, the famous African theologian, admits that the new evangelisation of Pope Francis is very different from past processes.[3] First of all, he points out that *Evangelii Gaudium* was born from criticism of the methodology of mission from secular sources, which has created a growing awareness of the dignity of individuals and peoples. And then he refers to the dualism created by the missionaries in Africa as: "The Error of the Two Distinct Publics in the Perception of Mission"[4]. He explains that the image of the "potted plant" as a model of evangelisation where Christianity was simply implanted or transplanted into the so-called pagan cultures or mission territories, should belong to the past. However, even about 60 years after Vatican

---

[2] V. ELIZONDO, *Evangelization is inculturation: A case study*, in *Missiology*: An International Review, 43/1(2015), 25. https://doi.org/10.1177/0091829614552632, (23/9/2021).

[3] *Ibid.*

[4] *Ibid.* meaning "the error of the two distinct audiences in the perception of the mission".

II, after realising that the methods of other times were unsustainable, many are still not convinced that inculturation in Africa should be considered an evangelisation. They still doubt the necessity of inculturation.[5] Magesa sees the new evangelisation as a call to critical solidarity, not just conversion. This means knowing the culture and sharing the good news with people through sincere dialogue. This is in fact what the synod on synodality suggests; it, therefore, requires a deep listening of African Christians and it should not be selective listening. Of course, it is a call to discernment about how the Holy Spirit wants us to lead evangelisation in Africa.

To understand Pope Francis in his actions, it would be good to know that he is indeed a pastor, not a "traditional theologian". It should be understood by this that, as a pastor, the Pope is more concerned with the sheep, than with theologising, for example, about how many angels can stand at the top of a needle. He can therefore identify himself with the needs of our time, for he himself smells the sheep. In elaborating on how evangelisers must walk with peoples through various popular devotions, the Holy Father indicates that we must have "the gaze of the Good Shepherd, who does not seek to judge but to love" (EG, 125). He concludes that this will happen not only through human efforts but also and above all through the manifestation of the Holy Spirit. In caring for the sheep, pastors in Africa have often noted how sheep are likely to oscillate between Christianity and African culture in ways that may seem incompatible. It is a question of double consciousness, a double identity which, in general, does not manage to "merge" to give way to an authentic African Christian identity, capable of fighting all the vices of tribalism, corruption and endless conflicts.

In fact, the pope focuses on the person, which is why in *Evangelii Gaudium,* he emphasises person-to-person dialogue in preaching, whether in Christian meetings or even in homilies. He is open to evangelisation, to possibilities such as personal testimonies, narratives and gestures... (cf. EG, 128). In Africa, aren't there a lot of symbols or signs that could be used? The Holy Father recognizes that the message of a person to a person can be different according to culture and that it can have limits. "If the Gospel is embodied in a culture, it is not only communicated through the proclamation of one person to another" (EG 129). This is not only for pastoral reasons, but it is an opportunity for theologians, whom *Evangelii Gaudium* calls to advance the dialogue on

---

[5] *Ibid.,* 18.

cultures and sciences, and not to "not be content with a desk-bound theology" (EG 133). To consider evangelisation as inculturation is a new way of accepting transformative inculturation. That is to say, a true inculturation that goes beyond simple biblical translations, simple liturgical symbols and dances and includes the global vision of the world and individual experience. Such an approach would help dispel the sceptical conceptions that continue to think that there is a hidden agenda behind evangelisation or Christianisation, especially those that link it to colonialism and crony capitalism.

Synod and Mission

Although there were no major changes, the synods often contributed to a new reflection on mission. The Second Vatican Council, for its part, had a significant impact on the evangelising mission of the Church, even though some reservations were expressed. The further we go, it seems to us that there is no great progress. In 1994, with the first African Synod, there was hope for a new African theology. But the 2009 Synod that followed, abandoned inculturation and opted for Reconciliation, Justice, and Peace, without yet clearly stating the methodology of the church to achieve it. However, our hope in the inspiration of the Holy Spirit remains firm.

This new synod, anchored on "participation, communion, and mission", seems to accentuate this hope for a renewal of our mission in the world. At the launch of the work of the Synod, Pope Francis spoke of the Synod as an encounter that flows from the journey together on the same path.[6] Jesus did not only preach; his Good News often came from rich encounters, such as with Zacchaeus and the Samaritan woman. These meetings were participatory: Zacchaeus opened up and accepted Jesus into his home; the Samaritan woman after she met with Jesus, went to the whole village to announce the good news. The sheep and the shepherd become one in participation and in the common mission. Our hope, in the face of the current management of the Covid-19 pandemic, which is marked by an individualistic and selfish nationalism, is that the mission leads to more fruitful meetings where missionaries can listen deeply to the voice and the cry of Africans.

---

[6] Cf. C. WELLS, "Pope: Celebrating Synod means walking together on the same road", in https://www.vaticannews.va/en/pope/news/2021-10/pope-celebrating-synod-means-walking-together-on-the-same-road.html, (18/10/2021).

Building African Christian identity through initiation

The main question is to see how traditional African cultural initiation from childhood to the majority, can be a tool for protecting African sheep of the sheepfold of Christ. Here we use the word initiation in the non-sacramental sense of baptism, communion, and confirmation, although they are not exclusive. It is no longer a secret that many young people do not participate in youth activities in parishes, because they are not meaningful to them. The same reason is given for the lack of membership in Catholic women's associations.

By focusing on young people, we discover that the frustrations they experience because of unemployment and possibly bad relationships require serious personal encounters with role models. It is only when young people can see Christ as the provider, the healer, the merciful, that they could remain in the fold. For very often Christ is seen superficially without strong conviction. That is why some will be able to receive it with the "blood of sacrifices" on their hands. Others are convinced that it is not powerful enough to free them.

The very useful and available cultural instrument is that of initiations. In Africa, children are usually initiated into adolescence or adulthood through rituals such as circumcisions (male and female). If they are properly integrated, as done in some dioceses in Kenya, young people can become a responsible age group, able to take charge of and support each other. This could create bonds and a sense of maturity, which is often lacking in today's world where many young people still live with their parents.

The lack of early transition initiations presents a challenge for many Catholic communities in Africa. In this sense, the Sacrament of Confirmation needs to be well inculturated, so as not to be just another formality to be completed in the Church; or even to avoid being reduced to fundraising for bishops' visits to parishes. A period of serious preparation for Confirmation and all the other sacraments is necessary. This must go beyond the few weeks or hours of preparation that we see in some dioceses. As a result of such superficiality, many young people simply fail to make the transition or the transition because they have been too much "cajoled". It also creates a void for the age group behind them. In some parishes, it is common to see adults in their late thirties, seeing themselves as young people and preventing adolescents from fully developing in the parish movements of their age group. These age groups should not be confused. For example, people over the age of 25 are often in a marriage situation and the image of Christ would be different from that of adolescents. Hence the need to adopt initiation programs according to age groups.

Conclusive implications of the new approach

A few implications could be drawn from the foregoing discussion. First, a renewed effort in the mission in Africa through sensitivity to interpersonal experience would motivate the activities of the Church as leaven. Moreover, missionary formation should not only be centred on culture, as it was in the past, but also on person-to-person dialogue. If we start from the "secular pressures", according to the expression of Magesa, which was the result of many calls for a dignified life for all, and which forced the new discourse of evangelisation as the foundation for the goals of sustainable development, then the missionary would be forced to consider the person and even outside his culture. So, when he identifies the cultural instrument, he can use it to build on individual experiences.

Secondly, rather than focusing on old-fashioned conversion, the emphasis must be placed on solidarity, considering people as capable of dialogue.

Third, as the Holy Father points out in *Evangelii Gaudium*, through the task of African theologians, who should demystify what seems to be anti-Christian, such as African prayers, which are often called charms or witchcraft, and other symbols that could easily be inculturated. In doing so people would feel Christianity close to them, and that it can respond concretely to the problems of their lives.

Fourth, missionary formation must consider not only the knowledge of cultures, but also those who live the conflict between culture and Christianity while continuing to seek the truth with sincerity.

Fifth, by seeing evangelisation as inculturation removes every form of superiority of the missionary, whether he is from the North or the South, the East or the West of the globe. The missionary would no longer strive, according to the warning of Bishop de Brésillac, to implant his home structures in others' homes.[7] Rather, he would become a mediator of Christ and his Good News. The missiologist Francis A. Oborji rightly points out that, far from being a church transplant, inculturation is the

---

[7] Cf. MARION BRESILLAC, *Mission and founding documents*, (Paris 1985), 88-89.

incarnation of Christ and his Gospel in a culture.[8] In this, the message of Christ will reach every human culture.

---

[8] Cf. F. A. OBORJI, *Trends in African Theology since Vatican II: A Missiological Orientation*, Leberit, Rome 2005², 94 – 95.

Confidence in collaboration as part of wisdom, the Original Wisdom

S. I. Francis Rozario SMA

Pope Francis started the synodal process in the Church with the words 'Participation, Communion, and Mission'. We have two years of preparation for the Synod. The three words 'Participation, Communion, and Mission' indicate that the *process* is more important than the *synod* itself. Two years of deliberations and mutual listening throughout the Church will bear a lot of fruit.

This article attempts to understand the wisdom of the synodal process by seeing it side by side with the way things work in the world. In the first part, we will see some of the changes in the society that are accepted, appreciated, and celebrated. In the second section, we will see how the attractive elements of the new changes reflect some basic elements of our understanding of God and nature. Then in the third section we will make some conclusions for our lived reality.

Changing music

"When the music changes, so does the dance". The music keeps changing in the world at various levels.

Classical model

Every organisation has a hierarchy, and every society has its leaders and experts. It is conventional to reserve certain knowledge, decisions, and their execution for leaders and experts. The idea behind this reservation is often (not always) well intentioned.

For national security, the military keeps some information as classified. To protect the right of innovators, and to maintain dominance, businesses keep technical and strategic information very private and reserved to top executives. Many religions like to keep the religious knowledge inaccessible to the public. In the olden days, the so-called sacred texts (Vedas) were reserved only to the priestly class in India. If a person of a lower caste hears the prayers, molten lead should be poured into his ears according to the norms established over 2000 years ago.[1] Whether or not the cruel punishment was ever executed, the rule sent a crystal-clear message and shows the desire of a group to jealously hold on to an exclusive knowledge. Christianity never taught anything that cruel but enjoyed the use of Latin for public liturgy that no layperson understood!!

Knowledge is power. Those who have access to information think for the society and decide for the society. But as both leaders and members of the society, can they be objective enough? History has an overabundance of examples, confirming the old maxim, '

'Power corrupts, and absolute power corrupts absolutely'.

Things stay under control when data stays under control. Public opinion, decisions, and culture are shaped through the control of data, information, and knowledge. Controlling data was widely understood as keeping it inaccessible to the majority so that a tiny minority could do the thinking and planning for everybody.

Changing trend

In recent years, we notice new trends behind the vocabulary like, 'public opinion', 'public domain', and 'open source'. What is behind the phenomenal growth of Google and Wikipedia? Here is the key - anybody can participate in improving them. Over 500 new articles are added by the general public everyday to Wikipedia.[2] Everybody can add

---

[1] "Now if he listens intentionally to (a recitation of) the Veda, his ears shall be filled with (molten) tin or lac." *Gautama Dharmasutra XII.4*, in WISDOM LIBRARY, https://www.wisdomlib.org/hinduism/book/gautama-dharmas%C5%ABtra/d/doc116312.html (accessed on March 29, 2022)

[2] WIKIPEDIA, "Wikipedia: Statistics", https://en.wikipedia.org/wiki/Wikipedia:Statistics#:~:text=While%20you%20rea

precisions to Google maps anytime from anywhere in the world. I added the photo and address of the SMA Generalate to Google maps. By doing so, I feel pleased with my contribution, visitors find our house more easily, and Google makes more money - not my primary intention!

If restriction was power, opening to the participation of others has become a greater power.

If holding on to information was power, spreading it out has become a greater power.

Any idea that remains locked up can become irrelevant and even be forgotten. An ideology is like a virus, it needs hosts for its own survival. Dominant ideas and ideologies are those shared by a vast number of people. Shaping public opinion has become an industry and a science today. People scramble to pass on information as much as possible. By the way, the Hindu Vedas are online today!

When more people think and act together, the output is far greater. Companies and organisations spend a lot of their resources on ensuring that people reflect together and participate in planning.

There is power when more people participate, and only smart and powerful people give access to others. By doing so, they become more powerful!

Something very interesting happened in the tech world last November. Jack Dorsey, the founder and CEO of Twitter resigned, not because of any problem but because of a principle. He wrote in his resignation letter, published in his official Twitter account, *"There's a lot of talk about the importance of a company being 'founder-led'. Ultimately, I believe that's severely limiting and the single point of failure."*

We see great wisdom here. People celebrate founders; and founders themselves feel attached to their brainchild projects. However, this attachment can limit the growth of the project and finally can even kill it.

The Original Music

The latest trends show wisdom. The trends are new, but the wisdom is not. The new music resonates with the original tune of life and the life-giver.

---

d%20this%2C%20Wikipedia,585%20new%20articles%20per%20day. (Accessed on March 29, 2022)

Creation

In Genesis 1: 26-27, we read about the creation of human beings. God shares his own image and likeness, and at the same time he shares the entire project with humanity: *"Then God said, 'Let us make humankind in our image, according to our likeness; and let them have dominion over the fish of the sea, and over the birds of the air, and over the cattle, and over all the wild animals of the earth, and over every creeping thing that creeps upon earth'"* (Gen 1: 26).

God makes humankind co-managers of the project at the point of creation itself!

Is God taking any risk by providing the admin access to human beings endowed with freedom, but are limited in knowledge? Are there real dangers? Cain kills his brother instead of being his guardian (Gen 4)! Unfortunately, the humanity has been living this story repeatedly. As I am writing this, Russia is on war against Ukraine and there are so many other wars and bloody conflicts all over the world. If this is what human beings do to their fellow human beings, how well can they take care of other species?

The human mind desires even to overthrow God and take His place as we see in the story of the tower of Babel - (Gen 11) and in the parable of the wicked tenants - *'This is the heir; come, let us kill him and get his inheritance.' (Mt 21: 38).* God takes a huge risk.

We are creative and productive and, by being so, we change the course of the creation in so many ways. God allows His project, his brainchild to be modified by us!

It takes real greatness to share power.

He made us co-managers not after training us but at our creation. God empowers humanity and starts mentoring. Here is the Original Wisdom!

Trinitarian relationship

The biblical texts about the three persons of the Trinity show how transparent they are to each other, how each one is handing over fully to the other, and how each one has full access to the other. Father gives 'all' He has to the Son (Jn 16: 15) and the Son hands over His life to the Father with absolute trust (Lk 26: 46). The Spirit has access to everything that belongs to the Son, and He takes them and discloses them to the disciples (Jn 16: 14).

We are created in the image and the likeness of the Triune God. If our life comes from the Trinity, the trinitarian model reveals the lifestyle that is life-giving. It reveals the real rhythm of life.

Mission of Jesus

We wonder sometimes why the ministry of Jesus was so short - just three years! Too short even for a parish priest! What would have changed if He had preached for thirty years instead of three? As an old man, He would have still commissioned his disciples to continue the mission. Well, He did exactly that at the end of His third year!

Jesus saw His mission as 'igniting a fire' (Lk 12: 49). This powerful metaphor reveals that the torch that is lit, lights others, those evangelised evangelise others, and those liberated liberate others. What matters more than the duration of a ministry is passing it on to the next generation.

How did Jesus begin His ministry?

By choosing His successors. (Mk 1: 16-20).

As Jesus began His ministry with the end game in sight, throughout his life He empowered the disciples by sharing all that He had. The disciples did not prove their worthiness or readiness, but Jesus empowered them and mentored them. Reflection of the Original Wisdom!

Sharing knowledge and skills

The most popular title given to Jesus was 'teacher'. He went around teaching - passing on knowledge. While other religions were busy mystifying simple things and separating the pure and the impure, Jesus lived revealing mysteries and died tearing down the veil that separated the Holy of Holies from the ordinary people.

Jesus called his disciples 'friends' because he made known to them everything he learnt from His Father (Cf. Jn 15: 15).

Not only did Jesus teach His disciples theoretical knowledge, but He also mentored them to do what He was doing. He sent them two by two on mission. He even told them that they could do greater works than He Himself (Cf. Jn 14: 12).

Sharing relationships

Apart from giving access to knowledge and skills - his 'public side', Jesus opened his most intimate space to the disciples. He prayed so that the disciples would be included in the intimacy he shared with the Father, *"Father, as you are in me and I am in you, may they be also in us" (Jn 17: 21)*

His friends became the friends of the disciples. The inclusive circle of friends kept growing. At the foot of the cross, He gave even His mother to the beloved disciple, saying, "Here is your mother", and after the resurrection, He said, "I am going to my Father and your Father". He sent out the Holy Spirit.

In short, He gave everything imaginable and even unimaginable - His body and blood.

The disciples shared the joy of communion with the entire network of Jesus.

Common mission

After giving everything, the mission of Jesus became the mission of the disciples. This is extremely interesting. Ordinarily servants carry out the mission of the master. The project usually belongs to the master and the servants work for a reward/salary.

In the case of Jesus, He called the disciples friends and shared everything with them. As a result, the mission of Jesus became the mission of the disciples. They continued the mission but not for a salary and despite persecution.

This passing on of mission became possible because He allowed them to participate in all that He had, and the disciples enjoyed communion with Him. Mission flows from that communion.

Checking our steps

Inspiring examples

We have a great number of outstanding examples not only in our history but also in many of our communities. The Sacred Heart hospital of Abeokuta in Nigeria was the very first hospital in the country. The whole project started with an inspiration to take care of the lepers of the place. The person behind the initiative was Fr. Justin François. His successor Fr. Coquard dedicated his entire life to the project, going far beyond the care of lepers.[3] The OLA sisters have continued to develop the hospital

---

[3] P. GANTLY, *Histoire de la Société des Missions Africaines (SMA) 1856-1907*, Tome 2, Paris 2010, 164.

over the years, and it is still serving the population today. Our history is full of such examples.

We see on the ground confreres who enjoy spending a substantial amount of time together for socialisation. Common meals and some common community activities play a key role. During these moments, they share a lot of information about their daily pastoral lives and every team member knows very well the things that happen in the others' areas. They are thus able to substitute each other seamlessly. Those who try to trick the priests, taking advantage of the absence of one, feel disappointed and surprised that all team-members are up to date with the issues involved.

In some places, we see confreres swapping the roles of the Parish Priest and the assistant after a few years in the mission and continuing to work together happily. They do not feel that they lose anything in the change of titles, and they see that their mission and their relationship continue to grow.

We see places where the Christian community is well informed and well empowered. The whole community enjoys a good service thanks to the deployment of the talents and expertise of its own members for the good of the Church. This reduces the work burden of the priest, brings more efficiency, and makes the administration more transparent. Priests and the laity feel mutually supported and consider their mission as their common commitment.

When we look at these good examples closely, we discover that the people involved have very good interpersonal relationships, the members feel a sense of inner security, and they all have a larger vision for mission. All these three points are significant. When they are lacking, we see examples of poverty. We sadly have lots of these too.

Examples of poverty

Some team leaders give the pastoral program and the timetable to other members of the team without any discussion. The leaders plan alone, content with their own share of wisdom, and generously make decisions for others. The team members, however, feel as if they are mere employees working for the project of the leader.

There are superiors who make various changes when the other members of the team are absent. When they come back, they can appreciate or criticise, but they cannot undo the changes! Smart strategy! We wonder whether the changes were done for the common good or for a personal satisfaction. If it is for the good of everybody, would it not make sense to plan that together? As soon as such people leave, their pet projects and their trademarks also disappear. If people with such a mindset succeed one another, each one will make his own personal dance and expect the people to applaud, a bit like everybody planting a new tree uprooting the old one and asking the people to water each successive one. They will water it but never harvest any crop! In this leadership style, where the superior alone makes the decisions, we see the wastage of common resources, the resentment of team members and the stagnation of the society.

Some prefer to have team members who are as non-threatening as possible (Remember we talked of the sense of inner security). Unfortunately, anything valuable can be threatening. Some go a step further and prefer team members who will be mere rubberstamps. They are chosen because of an obligation or a formality. Their names are there, but they are not involved in anything. They know nothing, and they do nothing. The leader alone does everything.

The desire to be surrounded by people who will never contradict us or oppose our ideas is like buying a car without brakes! It is not only a public danger but is also self-destructive.

It takes the strength of humility and wisdom to collaborate with more people, especially with those who know more than us and who are capable of more than we are. Real poverty results when people lack this capacity. Their personal limitations become the limitations of the public project entrusted to them.

Life is full of paradoxes and ironies

The grain of wheat must die before bearing fruit. The child must leave the mother's womb to grow into adulthood. The well needs to give out water to remain fresh.

What common conclusions about life can we draw from all this?

Giving without losing: Contrary to our fears, we do not lose by giving. Jesus did not lose His knowledge or relationships when He shared with the disciples. He did not retire when he commissioned the disciples. He did not lose His authority when He knelt down to wash their feet. Knowledge, relationships, and the mission can only grow to new heights.

Our gifts, dreams, and mission are greater than our space and time: Our lives are short and limited. We realise that we have various things to offer to the society for its continuous growth. Our gifts and dreams become relevant and meaningful in the context of the needs of the society. When the society recognises the positive impact of our gifts and contributions, it celebrates them in several ways. We understand that our gifts, dreams, and contributions are bearing fruit and the society finds them relevant. It is at this point that we have a choice, between carving out a space for ourselves only or ensuring that the society will continue to benefit from the contribution even beyond our time and space. This is the choice between what is pleasing to us at the superficial level and what is good for the project. Our own gifts and dreams need to go beyond us to be fruitful, like the child who will need to leave the mother's womb.

We innovate something because we change and modify something: It is this ability to change what was there before that becomes an innovation; it is the ability to move away from the tradition. If we want our initiatives to continue to grow, they need to go through many innovations in the future, which will mean changing from the original design. Founders and innovators like their projects and like all the details. They would be glad if others give continuity to their projects - without changing anything. This, however, is an unrealistic desire. Growth means change.

The projects that continue to be relevant are those which continue to change, adapt, and move beyond the original model. Happy are the founders and innovators who embrace this thought from the very beginning and let their projects grow beyond themselves.

Who is involved in this? This is not just for founders of institutions or companies, but for everybody who makes a valuable contribution to the society and wants the society to build on it instead of again going through the whole learning process of inventing a wheel. Ensuring continuity and promoting innovations are like two legs allowing one to march forward or even sprint.

Preparing a handover: Handover is one of the important procedures at the end of any important assignment. When is the best time to prepare for a handover?

We saw earlier that Jesus started his mission by choosing his successors. Our Founder planned his handover to the indigenous clergy before even going to the mission!

For us, limited mortals, succession planning is part of the mission. It is there right from the beginning to the end. When we work well as a team, with good interpersonal relationships, and transparency, as we saw in the examples above, another team member can take over seamlessly and continue to move forward.

How does that work when we do not know who the successor will be? Though we do not know who or what will follow, we know for sure that our journey in every area will end sometime. We need to pass on the knowledge and the value system not just to individuals but to the entire system. Successors emerge from a well-built system. They will already feel part of the tradition, and they will also innovate, making necessary and relevant changes.

We are talking here of a culture of transparency and a culture of inclusion. People in an organisation, parish, or a group need to know not only the decisions, but also the process that led to those decisions. They can know the process well only when they participate in the process. Everybody feels involved and included which is communion. They will then naturally own the common mission.

We might also wonder when we should pass on a project to our successors, especially when we are the initiators. Time is very relative! What matters is the wisdom of inclusion from the very beginning, knowing that we play a part in the journey of our society which will continue when our own journeys stop.

If you find something important,
share it!
If you have a mission,
pass it on!
If you love something,
let it go, and let it grow!

Spotlight: connecting with ...

... people seeking asylum
France

Daniel Cardot SMA

In the Society of African Missions, we have always emphasised that our mission is directed primarily to the most disadvantaged. Our founder already formulated it by asking us to exercise our mission among the most "abandoned of Africa". We have had to wait a long time for the term "peripheries" to be used, as Pope Francis now often does, but it amounts to the same idea. Our missionary family has always tried to be faithful to this mission, even if the diversity of situations has led us to exercise it in very different environments.

The SMA has also always declared, even in its Constitutions, that our mission is to be primarily exercised wherever Africans are present, not only in Africa itself, but also in our countries of origin. Thus, the Province of the United States has been involved for a long time with African-Americans and various commitments in the different Provinces or Districts have developed along these lines. As far as we in the Province of Lyons are concerned, it is the growing phenomenon of migration from Africa to Europe from the 1960s onwards that has helped us to recognise our mission as important in our country of origin as in Africa.

In a text written on the occasion of the "SMA day of reflection: *"Laudato si" and "Green spaces"* of November 7, 2020, we read: "We missionaries are heirs of the encounter between two continents: Europe and Africa. As Christians and as an International Society, do we not have a prophetic word to announce to renew the bonds of brotherhood today?"

Looking for a commitment

In 2001, after twelve years in Rome, the Provincial Council asked me to look for a missionary commitment in Lyons, with priority given to Africans. After contacts with the local Church several possibilities of commitment presented themselves. Based on the experience I had acquired with Africans in difficult situations in Paris between 1977 and 1981 as a volunteer in the Association ATD (Act Together for Dignity) Fourth World, I committed myself from 2002 to 2015 with the 'Asylum Seekers Reception' (*Accueil des Demandeurs d'Asile* - ADA), one of the branches of Caritas (*Secours Catholique*) in Lyons.

Before that, in the 1970s and 1980s, Jean Thébault and I were involved in the ATD Fourth World Association. At that time, in Paris, we mainly met Africans working in difficult jobs: assembly line work in automobile factories or as garbage collectors for the Paris city administration. Others were unemployed, others still (individuals, families, or single mothers) in great financial difficulty, gradually cut off from their original environment and isolated in society. We met them sometimes in the workplace but mostly in migrant hostels. Some of these centres at that time were very dilapidated. Sometimes the beds were used in "three shifts": three people used the same bed for eight hours each. This has improved over the years; new centres have been built. Sometimes we also met in large rooms reserved for the PMU (*Pari Mutuel Urbain*, where people bet on horse races in front of a large number of television sets) or in other communal recreational settings.

I would like to recount my experience of a time I spent with a Malian garbage collector: I am sharing it with you as I wrote it at the time, as an example of a bond which was established:

"Sissoko (the few names mentioned in this document are pseudonyms), originally from Mali, had been in France for 12 years. He spoke very little French. That was why he was taking part in literacy classes that I had organised with a group of students in two migrant hostels in the 19th arrondissement of Paris. For several years, he had been suffering from shoulder pain which was becoming an anxiety. In fact, he was a garbage collector for the city of Paris and, feeling these pains increasing, he had already had to take a few days off work to rest and for the pain to ease. He was dreading the moment when he would have to leave his job. It was becoming increasingly difficult for him to lift the bins. And how could he continue to support his family back home who were waiting each month for the money to live on?

- But go see a doctor, Sissoko, "I said. - No," he replied. The dialogue stopped at this point for months on this subject. Then one day he said to me: "Do you know a doctor who speaks Sarakolé? - No, but a friend could translate. A few days later we met again, and I told him: "I know a doctor friend in whom I have complete confidence. - When are we going to see him? And this doctor, what treatment does he use? Does he only look at your body? I asked him to trust me, especially since this doctor had worked for years in Africa.

We made an appointment with the doctor friend. Sissoko wanted me to stay with him for the whole consultation. Dialo, a mutual acquaintance, accompanied us to translate. I stood in a corner. The doctor talked for a long time with his patient, who had the chance to explain what he was feeling.

The consultation lasted an hour. Sissoko relaxed and unwound in front of a man for whom he was not just a body, because previously he had been afraid that the doctor would not consider what he was going through inside. At the end, as I was leaving, the doctor said to me: "I am not completely sure if the treatment I am giving will work; this kind of pain can have several causes. If the pain continues, we will look at it again. Whatever about the correctness of the treatment, I can testify that it was effective to the point that Sissoko was able to resume and keep his job and constantly asked me to return with him to the doctor, "only to thank him". Which we did. The doctor told me later: "It is not possible that only the medicine had this effect so quickly." But in Africa we know that medicine alone does not cure.

For asylum seekers

So here I am now, twenty years later (from 2002 to 2015), a member of the ADA team in Lyons, a team committed to asylum seekers. The circumstances of these types of migrants was unknown to me. I did not distinguish it properly from other forms of migration and in particular from the economic migration I had experienced twenty years earlier in Paris. So I had to find out who those were who came to France to obtain refugee status. I did this thanks to a quite extensive ongoing training at the beginning and then regularly thereafter, thanks also of course and primarily to the many regular meetings with asylum seekers themselves, sometimes individual meetings, sometimes in families or groups, and also thanks to the many day-to-day conversations with each member of the team, each one feeling the need to process together what we were experiencing.

The asylum application

An asylum seeker is a person who seeks protection in a country other than his or her own, even though in that country he or she is in danger, often even in danger of death, and in any case without the possibility of living freely and being protected there. But this person has not yet been recognised as a refugee in the country to which he has come. He or she has to go through long (the time limits have since shortened) and rather complex procedures to obtain refugee status. Migrants, refugees and asylum seekers have rights protected under international law. In principle they enjoy the same rights as any other human being, as well as, in some cases, specific protections, as expressed in Article 14 of the Universal Declaration of Human Rights: "Everyone has the right to seek and enjoy in other countries asylum from persecution". The word "persecution" does not necessarily have the religious connotation that it most often has for us. It can be political, social, cultural or religious persecution. Now there are also victims of climate change, but I have not known asylum seekers in this kind of situation. It seems to be becoming more common these days.

By meeting with asylum seekers, we gradually discover that the causes that push them to leave are multiple.

Causes of the claim

The reasons for claiming refugee status can be grouped under six headings: (all examples below refer to specific individuals encountered)

Persecution because of **race.** An example: a Sudanese man, Nubian by origin, who campaigned for the preservation and revival of Nubian culture by creating an association that promoted the Nubian language, literacy in this language, and a nascent literature; this man was put in prison as acting against the unity of the country, which only recognizes the Arabic language. He escaped (this was during the war in Darfur) and fled abroad.

Because of **religion.** For example: people, Christian or Muslim, who have fled their country for fear of being forcibly enrolled in the traditional religion, sometimes in what is called a "convent", or because they had been consecrated to the spirits by their parents; or a Muslim wanting to become a Christian threatened with death.

Because of **nationality.** An example: during political crises in certain countries, people, families, are forced to flee because it is impossible to return to the country where they were living, sometimes they are not recognised as nationals of that country. This concerns above all a fairly large number of people living in the republics of the former USSR; people born to parents of different nationalities (for example, one is Armenian and the other Ukrainian); before independence, when the USSR ceased to exist, they were all citizens of the USSR. Now these people are not recognised as citizens by any country. The countries send them back and forth to each other and the people have to choose a third country where they have to process their papers.

Because of belonging to certain **social groups.** For example: families from one ethnic group are, from father to son, at the service of a master from another ethnic group, without any autonomy, without any remuneration in money, but only the bare necessities of life, clothes, housing, food. Young people refuse to live in the way their parents had done which they consider slavery. They are put in prison if they protest. Or people who are subjected to forced marriage...

Because **of political views.** For example: opponents of the regimes in place in certain countries or during a change of regime, or during civil or international wars. We also often meet civil servants, soldiers or students who have fought against corruption or who have denounced abuses of power by the police or the administration, who have campaigned for the rights of peasants or belonged to an association for the defence of human rights, and who, persecuted, have seen their lives and those of their families endangered, sometimes, and quite often, to the point of death.

Now there are also victims of climate change, which is a new reality that I have not experienced.

It is often the case with asylum seekers that the economic and political reasons for leaving home are very intertwined. However, "refugee" status cannot be granted for economic reasons: economic distress is not considered as "persecution". The conditions for obtaining residence on economic grounds are very strict and different from those for an asylum application; these conditions must be fulfilled even before leaving their country. Many people who cannot meet these conditions look for reasons other than economic to be accepted. They are usually rejected because they cannot provide evidence of "persecution". However, even if their application is rejected, the vast majority of them have valid reasons for leaving their country. Leaving your country is not a smooth or easy process. Some of them have even been abused, the traces of which can still be seen on their bodies, but they cannot prove the origin of these scars. A significant number die on the way. This is why the vast majority, once their application for asylum has been rejected, do not want to or, for some, cannot return to their country. Some risk death, others refuse to go back to live in the same conditions as before, or consider that they cannot give up after having travelled such a difficult path. Some would like to go back, but they cannot return empty-handed. The first reaction of a Congolese man who had just learned that his application had been rejected by OFPRA (French Office for the Protection of Refugees and Stateless Persons) was to say to me, holding his head in his hands: "And I am the one who sold my family's plot of land in the village to come here. The family will be completely unable understand if I go back like this; I'll be rejected. This is why many asylum seekers, who have to leave French territory after being notified that their application has been rejected, refuse to go back. They become undocumented migrants, now illegal who constantly try to escape from the police.

Support for asylum seekers

Our activity at ADA consisted first of all of listening to people and then of accompanying them through the asylum application procedure, with all that this implies in terms of time for sharing, and various approaches to the administration or to other associations or to physical or psychological health services. First of all, we get to know the person concerned and then, very quickly (because of the deadlines imposed) we help him/her, if he/she wishes, to put together an account of the circumstances and causes that led him/her to apply for asylum, a story that the person must send and then present personally in Paris to OFPRA in order to obtain refugee status. Of course, this "story" must correspond to the criteria for asylum and therefore must concern a proven persecution. In this work, trust grows as we become familiar with each other and the person becomes more and more explicit. This requires a sufficiently long period of accompaniment, listening and then writing, as the person does not reveal everything on the first day and the data can be modified by the contribution of new data from the country (in particular proof of the risks taken if the person returns to his/her native country while taking into account the strict deadlines required by the administration. This account must be very detailed and accompanied by as many documents as possible proving the veracity of what has been written: diaries, medical records, other evidence or testimonies from the country itself. These exchanges about the "story" lead to other steps, especially concerning health, the resources needed to live, housing for individuals or families, and the search for places or groups that will allow the beginning of social integration. Often it is necessary to call upon other associations.

The vast majority of asylum seekers find themselves in a difficult material and psychological situation when they arrive in France. Often the conditions of travel to France are very trying. In most cases, at least for a large number of people who have had to cross the Sahara, the person has had to earn a living along the way, in particular to pay the smugglers but also simply to survive, which may have led some to spend up to three or four years in different countries along the way. The small resources at the start (sometimes the whole family has contributed) are quickly exhausted... Then you arrive in a country where you don't know anyone, where you have no human or even geographical reference. In some cases, you don't even know which country you have arrived in. Moreover, they have often come illegally, without a visa or even a passport, with all the complications that this implies for everyday life until they obtain a certificate of residence that allows them to begin the procedures required for refugee status. This arrival is therefore a shock that does not correspond at all to the hopes that one had placed in this lifechanging project. For many, at the beginning, this hope was very high.

At ADA, the choice has been made to receive and accompany mainly single people or people who have come without their families, because families are better taken care of by the State, they are followed up more closely in the Transit Centres and by the Red Cross. But there are exceptions. Sometimes we work with families, especially when the process was started by a single person who was then joined by family members.

This support requires extensive ongoing training and involves working with lawyers, government departments, psychologists, and other associations such as, in our case in Lyons, Forum Réfugiés (refugee forum), La Cimade, the Red Cross, etc. This also requires participation in mixed (public-private) commissions. For example, I took part in the "Concerted Admission Authority", which includes civil servants from the administration (especially from the Prefecture) and members of associations dealing with the allocation of accommodation to asylum seekers living on the street. This is what I wrote in 2009 after a meeting of the Commission: "At present, there are still many people who cannot find accommodation. In our department alone there is a list of 120 people waiting for accommodation in Lyons and we are not the only ones working in this area; at the meeting there were 6 associations and each one has a waiting list. Every week, in our meetings with the Prefecture officials, we obtain between 4 and 7 accommodation places for these 120 people. A good number of these people, many of whom live on the street, use the 115 service (emergency accommodation service), which can accommodate someone for between one and four nights. Often the 115 has no more places to offer. Sometimes private individuals or religious communities are called in, especially in difficult cases, the priority being accommodation for homeless pregnant women. A clear contract is then drawn up with the individuals or the community for a period of a few days to 15 days. Then we have to find another place to stay, as the hosting is done in rotation.

As an example, here is another (abbreviated) account of an afternoon spent at the reception desk highlighting the various difficulties encountered and the issues to be resolved (this is from 2003):

"I met seven people this afternoon including:

Two people from Congo Kinshasa, including a father of 6 accused of being linked to opposition forces and facing prison; he is asking for help with his 'story'.

A person from Congo Brazza who sleeps mostly at the Perrache station when he is ill: he is looking for safer accommodation.

A person, a Christian from Iraq, without papers, in France for two years, who is not entitled to any subsidy, nor housing, nor work; she speaks of a situation of death.

Two people from Albania wanted for participating in democratic demonstrations. They do not know where to go.

A man from Uzbekistan, persecuted for being non-Muslim; he is looking for accommodation.

Here is another note taken at the end of another half day that clearly indicates that each person is in a different situation (in 2006):

"Steps taken today: Listening to each person and their current problems: living on the street, loneliness, feeling powerless, fatigue, illness, unpaid bills, contact made with a lawyer for an appeal but which cannot be pursued due to lack of money (when OFPRA has refused refugee status, an appeal can be made to a Commission des Recourses, but new elements must be brought in and a lawyer must be consulted), difficulties in moving forward with the regularisation process as the process seems very complicated. After listening, we tried to move forward with the different steps (story, appeal, re-examination, then various contacts with associations to meet these different needs).

Different steps in the refugee status process

Each person we met was at a specific stage in the asylum application process. There are several stages: obtaining a residence permit (Prefecture), approaching OFPRA, then, if refused, approaching the Appeals Commission, then, if refused again, applying for a re-examination. The proportion of acceptances and refusals has varied greatly over the years. I have experienced a level of granting of status ranging from 18 to 40% of applications, depending on the period. A few examples highlight the stage each person is at:

"Mrs X (Iraq): there are still two months to go before the lawyer can hope to trace the documents that will allow her to appeal to the Commission for a re-examination. As she has been in France for two years and the first appeal was refused, she is in an illegal situation... She has to wait, all the while fearful of receiving an Obligation to Leave French Territory before obtaining the documents necessary for the re-examination.

Mr X (Angola): He is waiting for a reply to the appeal he sent to the ad hoc committee. He has had no resources since June (it is October). For food, he goes to the Protestant Solidarity, the *Resto du cœur* (an association that offers free meals) and the Red Cross. It is easier to find food than accommodation. He lives illegally in a SONACOTRA shelter (lodging provided for construction workers) with a friend. His wife and child are still in Eastern Europe.

Mrs X (Armenia): in France for several years. She was refused by OFPRA. She is therefore in the appeal process. She has already appeared before the Appeal Commission. The latter has just sent her a letter saying that the answer is postponed. For the appeal process, she had to pay a large sum to the lawyer (at that time the lawyer was not appointed), she no longer has sufficient resources.

Mrs X (Congo Kinshasa): received the APS (*Autorisation Provisoire de Séjour* – Temporary residence permit) from the Prefecture today. She must send her story and her asylum application to OFPRA within a month. She says she will finish writing it tomorrow. She will bring it to me so that we can review it together before sending it. In her country, she was imprisoned and abused after being arrested for attending meetings of an opposition party. She has been in France for a few months and still has no accommodation. She asks for addresses to find warm clothes. We give her some.

Mrs X (Congo Kinshasa). She has just obtained refugee status, directly from OFPRA itself, which is very rare, as most of the time we have to wait for the Appeal Commission, which grants up to 20%. Great joy, hope is reborn. She lives at the Point-Nuit. She could perhaps apply for the RMI (*Revenu Minimum d'Insertion* – minimum income for social insertion). We are going to take the necessary steps with her to obtain the "*Aide pour la Vie de Tous les Jours* (Assistance for everyday living)" from Caritas, for the critical period before she enters the French administrative circuit.

Mr. X (R.C.A.): Wants to tell his story. He hasn't eaten since yesterday. I go with him to a grocery store.

Mr X (Algeria). Obtained his document granting permission to reside in France to apply for asylum. Trader in Algeria. He has had problems with the G.I.A (Armed Islamic Group). He spent 5 years in Libya where he worked to pay a smuggler. OFPRA rejected his application, so he has to appeal. He asks us to help him.

Mr X (Sierra Leone): has not received a response from OFPRA. There was a problem with his address because he lives on the street. We provide him with a direct debit from Caritas, which we do for homeless people so that they can receive their mail.

When the person has obtained refugee status, hope is reborn. But it still takes months of hard work to find housing and work, and a gradual insertion into human groups and, for Christians, into the Church. Here again, we have to find ways of directing these people to the various places where they can find answers to their various problems. As for those who have not obtained this status, after having gone through all the possible stages, if they do not return to their country, and it is rare that they do, they enter the informal world of the undocumented, whether it be for housing, work or social life, with all that this implies.

Evaluation

After twelve years of working with asylum seekers, it is difficult to make an assessment. We regularly took stock of the situation in the team, in addition to the training sessions. But it would be up to the people concerned to take stock. It is difficult to know what has happened to all those whose search for refugee status has failed. A minority have returned home. Others have tried procedures in another country. Others have remained in France and live under various statuses, either illegal or, after a number of years, legalised.

But we can still see some results: links with asylum seekers have been created. A certain number of people have found their place in society and in their respective communities, they have found work and started a family. Some Christians have found their place in a parish (for many, however, integration into the local Church is very difficult).

And above all, what we were able to realize is that through the meetings, many prejudices fell away, mentalities changed. First of all, we ourselves, the members of the team, discovered a world that we only knew through reading or News. In the people we met, we often found cultural elements that some of us had known in Africa. But the context is so different that it changes everything in how the people live and in the relationships that this creates. But at least this world of a thousand faces has broadened our own horizons, our knowledge and our outlook.

In the same way, on the part of the people we have welcomed and accompanied, sometimes for years, we have witnessed changes in outlook and behaviour that are sometimes surprising. Just two examples to illustrate this. An Algerian asylum seeker, Mohamed, a fundamentalist of the FIS (Islamic Salvation Front), who made no secret of it, even if only in his clothes and words, after four weeks of meetings and discussions about his "story" for OFPRA, which we were preparing together at his request, invited one of his friends (accompanied by his little boy) to take part in the next meeting. This is rare because, when preparing a story, the exchange contains a lot of confidential data and great discretion must be maintained. When I asked the friend why he had come to this meeting, he replied: "Mohamed said to me: 'Come and see something we don't know: there are Christians who love us Muslims'. In previous meetings we had never spoken about our respective religions. He only knew that we were linked to Catholic Relief Services and therefore that we were Christians. Another reaction: a Congolese man, after a long journey together in the administrative process and then during a long stay in the hospital where I was visiting him, said to me: "I thought I had been bewitched, I was certain that I was under bad influences and even that I had been poisoned... My steps with you have delivered me from these thoughts. Even today, he still calls me, talks to me about his work, about the family he was able to build (in 2021, I am still in touch with many of those I met in 2002).

The migration issue raises very different opinions and commitments

Anyone who is involved in activities concerning migrants is aware that this kind of involvement arouses criticism, sometimes even strong opposition. We know that the question of migration in all its forms (especially economic migrants, asylum seekers and refugees) is a major concern in our country. We are well aware that there are very different positions regarding this situation and that this leads to opinions, projects and activities that are sometimes opposed to each other.

We also know that the migration issue requires political decisions and that the problems raised are real and serious, that these decisions are not obvious or easy to take and to put into practice, and that they are never universally accepted. We know that there is pressure at the borders. We know that there are those who would like to see a very strict policy of limiting migration. We know that the need for a certain amount of labour, on the other hand, leads others to seek out and welcome foreigners into Europe, especially to do jobs that no one in the country wants to do. We know that Africa is in danger of losing a vital part of its population and that a very broad international organisation is needed to ensure that this continent has the necessary means to avoid this human haemorrhage. We are well aware of the risks and fears that this migratory issue rouses in several areas, political, economic, cultural and religious. It is necessary that these questions be asked, and solutions found. But, at our level, we do not claim to answer global political and economic questions, even if we are convinced that we have a role to play.

How do we place our mission in this context?

In our modest role as ordinary citizens, but also as Christians and missionaries, how can we participate in this search for solutions? We see the reality, we see what is happening: Africans, men, women and children, therefore brothers and sisters in humanity, are there. There are even many of them in France and a good number of them have experienced and continue to experience serious unjust treatment. Discrimination exists, racism is still frequent, certain social tensions are alarming. We note that human groups of different origins, in this case Africans and Europeans, often live in parallel, maintaining a reciprocal ignorance that leads to prejudice against each other and misunderstandings with numerous and sometimes serious consequences. This contradicts what we believe about man: everyone loses. We can see that it is possible to move forward towards greater connection, towards living together. We have already tasted some of the fruits of this in our own lives and it has allowed us to evolve, to move forward in our search for a shared life.

So, in this context, we choose to walk together, to go to meet the other, to welcome him and to let him welcome us, to believe that making this journey is an enrichment to be achieved, we think that this is to what our faith and the conception of man that it gives us call us. In this choice and in connection with others, we try to live the universalism proposed by the Gospel, to refuse to withdraw into ourselves. We are among those who want to create links, build bridges, participate in the search for solutions to the difficulties of everyday life, to the trials that our migrant brothers and sisters are going through, starting from the Gospel values of welcome, respect and love for every human person. This must of course be done taking into account the society in which they come to live, and this is certainly not easy. But it is only together, with them, that we will build something worthwhile. We know that the challenge is difficult to meet, but we believe in it without being naive because we have already experienced certain aspects of it.

Pope John Paul II said: "The spirit of solidarity is not spontaneous. It requires a deepening of roots and a move away from the attitudes of withdrawal which, in many societies today, have become more subtle and entrenched. To address this phenomenon, the Church has many resources for education and formation at all levels. This is why I call on parents and teachers to combat racism and xenophobia by instilling positive attitudes based on Catholic social teaching." Pope Francis extends to the whole of society what his predecessor said to educators: "Greater attention and support must be given to migrants, asylum seekers and refugees with disabilities". And he underlined the "great responsibility" of each one with regard to the migrant: "Every immigrant who knocks at our door is an opportunity for an encounter with Jesus Christ, who identifies himself with the foreigner of every era, welcomed or rejected.

Living the mission of the Church today in connection with the local Church

In order to live the missionary life in direct connection with the diocesan Church, during these same years spent in Lyons, in addition to the ministry with the African world, I accepted other commitments that were in line with our vocation to the most needy: in addition to the commitment with the ADA, I assumed in Lyons the role of diocesan chaplain of Caritas for years, and from 2013 to 2017 I took on the responsibility of visiting patients at the end of life in the framework of the chaplaincy of two hospitals in Lyons including the military hospital Desgenettes. I also joined the prison chaplaincy team at the Corbas prison near Lyons to visit the prisoners. Christians from a wide variety of churches came to the prison chaplaincy (mostly African but not only) and sometimes some Muslims. There were groups of about twenty people. On Saturdays we prepared for the Eucharist which we celebrated on Sundays, and during the week we had a "talking group". This time of discussion gave the prisoners a unique opportunity to talk about their own history, about what was happening in the prison, about certain events outside the prison that they had heard about on the radio or television. One day, at the end of a meeting between women prisoners, when the guard came to unlock the door of the room where we were (the meeting lasted two hours) to say that the meeting was over and to order us to leave, one of the women said to me: "I had forgotten that we were in prison, this knock on the door reminds me of it". Even if we were not there to make people forget reality, this reflection showed the interest that people had in participating in these meetings.

In 2020, Pope Francis, on the occasion of World Migrants Day, wrote: "During the flight to Egypt, the Child Jesus experiences, together with his parents, the tragic condition of displaced person and refugee characterised by fear, uncertainty, inconvenience"... "Today, unfortunately, millions of families can recognize themselves in this sad reality. Almost every day, television and newspapers carry news of refugees fleeing from hunger, war and other grave dangers, in search of safety and a dignified life for themselves and their families. In each one of them, Jesus is present, forced to flee to save himself, as in the time of Herod. In their faces we are called to recognize the face of Christ, hungry, thirsty, naked, sick, a stranger and a prisoner, who calls out to us (cf. Mt 25: 31-46). If we recognize him, it is we who will thank him for us having been able to meet him, love him and serve him."

Conclusion

The Directory of the Province of Lyons N°106 tells us: "It is important that confreres and communities be open and welcoming to migrants, especially those from Africa, in connection with the pastoral work of the local Church and with the help of organisations that help migrants. (AP 2019 p.19)." It is with joy that we can see this affirmation taken seriously and put into practice whether in the parishes entrusted to us in France or in our communities where several confreres are directly involved in this important mission. The mission continues. Praise be to God!

... people at a leprosarium Ivory Coast

Francis Athimon SMA

The leprosarium of Adzope

Their world

During the year 2016, my Provincial Superiors in Lyons, for my 75th birthday, suggested that I take up the post as the Catholic Chaplain at the Leprosarium of Adzopé in Ivory Coast. I knew almost nothing about this place and the people who lived there. But I accepted, considering that my health was quite good and that I could be quite independent. I did a little research, before leaving, on leprosy, on the ethnic group that was there and the language spoken, Attié. I even managed to get a book on the Attié and the Attié-French dictionary typed out in an ordinary notebook by Fr. Margerit, found in the library in Lyons 150.

I arrived there on November 8, 2016, and was very warmly welcomed. I had a proper installation such as for a Curé by the Episcopal Vicar Father Pacôme Ndende who is at the same time Curé of the Parish of St Charles Borromée in Adzopé. This parish was founded in 1939 by Father Miet SMA. And he also created the leprosarium of Adzopé, because he wanted very much to take care of the lepers, he even looked after them himself. The Director General of the IRF (Institut Raoul Follereau de Côte d'Ivoire, the official name of the hospital which means

Raoul Follereau Institute of Ivory Coast), Professor Vagamon Bamba, was present at the installation, along with doctors from the Medical Corps, nursing and maintenance staff and patients who could move around. The inhabitants of the nearby village of Duquesne-Cremone also came. A renovated presbytery was ready and I moved in immediately. The 3 OLA Sisters who live there and are nurses in the hospital invited me to eat with them for 2 months before I got my own kitchen organised. So I definitely felt like I was welcomed as the "Messiah". In fact, my predecessor as Chaplain of the IRF had died at the beginning of March 2015 so they had been almost 2 years (20 months exactly) without a chaplain. But perhaps some were secretly worried because I was told 4 years later that there was a patient who, as I was "a white man", was afraid that I would cut off his head. An old ancestral fear that goes back to the beginning of colonisation, which we know was sometimes cruel. Father J.P. Eschlimann explains this.

So, once I got settled, I set about trying to find out what the IRF was all about. First of all, there are the patients, as we officially prefer to call them. There are 170 inpatient beds and it's pretty much always full. But now that leprosy has diminished considerably, only 60 to 70 Hansenians are treated, mainly for complications or after-effects of the disease which cause wounds on the feet and hands that are difficult to heal. Then there are the Buruli ulcer patients. This is a disease which also causes serious and life-threatening wounds. There are many other conditions that produce large wounds: diabetes, motorcycle, and car accidents, burn victims, hemiplegics with bedsores and cancer patients who are operated on for tumours on their arms or legs. They treat anything that causes major wounds. A dozen doctors come to take care of these patients. They don't live in the area. They stay either in Adzopé city, which is 12 km away along an unpaved track, or in Abidjan. They are assisted by nurses. The staff includes pharmacists, laboratory assistants, nurses' aides, cooks, maintenance personnel, security guards and drivers. The others are in the administration: the DG with his secretaries, the DAF Director of Financial Affairs, the accountants, the electricians, and the water department. The operating theatre operates 3 days a week. Patients are often accompanied by one or two people who take care of them. The hospital is therefore a hive of activity containing at least 300 people, even if not everyone is present at the same time. Every Sunday afternoon I visited the different wards where the patients have their beds.

Apart from the hospital, there is, in my pastoral assignments, the nearby village called Duquesne-Cremone which has almost 3000 inhabitants. It has a diverse population: the workers of the IRF who live there, former lepers who have been cured along with their families. It is they who wanted to create this village because they were stigmatised in their native villages and did not want to return. Finally, as we are in the forest zone, cocoa planters came to settle there. There are also some Dioula traders. There is a primary school with 500 pupils, a dispensary, a maternity hospital with more than 80 births in a year, owners of cassava mills and coffee crushers. For all these people, there is a Catholic church, a mosque and several Evangelical and Protestant churches. And while I was there a new community was created in a forest camp called MAFOU and it called on my services to go there from time to time to celebrate Mass and the Sacraments. So this is what I found when I arrived in 2016 and which I left in 2021. It would be worthwhile for a proper history of this hospital for lepers to be compiled. Here I will only put on record that it was Fr. Miet who started this centre for the cure of leprosy. He was helped, from 1941, by Sister Eugenia, Superior General of the OLA Sisters at that time. The first leprosarium was only 3 km from the town of Adzopé. The inhabitants objected, however, considering the patients as living too close to them so they had to go 12 km into the forest to build another place. Work began in 1948, and by 1951 more than 200 lepers had already been treated. Raoul Follereau was totally committed to the cause and found funds. The OLA Sisters were responsible for the running of the centre as few people were willing to come and work in this context. In 1971, President Houphouet Boigny officially named this hospital Institut Raoul Follereau (IRF) and financially supported its operation.

The ideas that are current in this special place

As is often the case in Africa, illness of any kind is often seen as a bad spell caused by an enemy. And when a third party is needed to treat the illness the first person to be contacted is the traditional healer, who is often referred to as a witch doctor. Sometimes a rogue witchdoctor approaches people trying to make them believe that they are threatened by all sorts of danger and that they need to protect themselves. All this means that, when there is a serious illness, there is often a delay before the patient is brought to the hospital for treatment. It takes a lot for the traditional mentality to be transformed by a modern scientific mindset. Evangelisation sometimes contributes to further the misconceptions by making people believe that praying to Jesus will also heal everything. Certainly, the doctors and staff believe in their therapies and seek to improve them, but they also believe in the need for spiritual or mystical forces to promote healing. There are surgeons who pray before surgery. And I have witnessed the enthusiastic success of charismatic style prayers performed by promoters of this method.

Another difficulty is that it is well known that leprosy or contagious diseases such as COVID cause an unreasonable fear of those who show symptoms. And this leads to an attitude of rejection or flight from these people. This is what has caused cured lepers, "cleared" as they say, to prefer to create their own village rather than return to their native villages. Fortunately, this stigmatisation is diminishing as the sick are more and more looked after by healthy family members. And now many other wounds are also treated alongside leprosy. But leprosy patients still have the tendency to hide their infirmities with shoes or gloves which they remove as soon as they are no longer in public or exposed to public life.

As in all human places, all kinds of illicit and illegal traffic take place. The medical profession itself does not hesitate to ask for extra money so as to benefit financially from the use of their expertise. The same is true with medicines. There are also drugs, cannabis, alcohol in bags of 20 grams, cannabis, prostitution, robberies, etc... Sometimes the police come to arrest a criminal. Even the security guards are not above suspicion, as I know from personal experience having been robbed by one of them. Sometimes the lower paid staff come to me to complain about not having received their salary for several months.

The social implications

The result of these attitudes is that people are seen as being in different categories and at different social levels. There are special units where the patient has a single or double room with air-conditioning and ensuite toilet facilities. Others are hospitalised in common rooms where there are up to 18 beds squeezed together. The children who are there cannot go to school. The treatment is long: 6 months, 1 year, sometimes 2 years or more. And then there are the girls or boys who are there to help the sick members of their family. Apart from the work in the kitchen, the washing of dressings and the sheets, they are free, even idle. There is no one to take care of them. The lepers who are able to leave the hospital regularly go to beg on Fridays at the Mosque in Adzopé. They often have no other monetary income and are dependent on donations of clothes to dress themselves and soap to wash themselves. Such irradicable poverty forces them to be permanently dependent on charity. Since they are sometimes handicapped, it is difficult for them to do manual work such as farming or preparing food. Life is difficult for those having to use prostheses, walking sticks, crutches, and wheelchairs. Even in the village of Duquesne-Cremone, there are differences in levels. The old men and women do not always have enough to eat. The Sisters distribute food to the neediest every week. I even saw some of them, when they died, being buried without a coffin.

On the other hand, the farming population works and is able to provide for its own needs. It is not uncommon to see solar panels, satellite dishes and therefore television and the possibility of recharging mobile phones. They organize parties especially on the occasion of religious events e.g. baptisms or weddings. The women are well dressed and wear jewellery. Some of them play an important role in the administrative or political authorities. Thus I am in contact with two very different contrasting worlds.

Building bridges

What has been done: pastoral initiatives

The primary role of the chaplain, of the priest, is to gather a community together either to pray the Mass or the Sacraments, or to conduct funerals. Priests also teach e.g. catechism to prepare adults and young people for baptism or for marriage. In the hospital, in my own house, I taught catechism to three or four sick people every year. They came two afternoons a week. The teaching was in French, which they more or less understood but I noticed that they did not know how to read, not even the young ones. It is difficult to follow an effective teaching program. I also had some adults from the medical profession, with whom I could have a proper dialogue. In the Duquesne-Cremone village and out in the fields, there were catechists, particularly the sisters in the recent years. This then made it necessary to organize the formation of the catechists with two all-day meetings per quarter. These were enriching meetings because there was dialogue, questions, and answers. Learning to analyse the environment, customs, mentalities and fears, helps to make people aware of what is an obstacle to the Gospel, but also of all that is compatible with the message of Jesus. Another place to deepen the faith and the Christian existence is the BCC (Basic Christian Communities) as it is organised in the Ivory Coast. After much effort, a group has been established in Duquesne-Cremone. For the children, apart from the catechism or the choirboys, it was the CV-AV movement (Catholic Action for Children) that worked. Young women and boys, already adults, were leading this movement. It was a pleasure to see. Thanks to the Sisters, the women also started an organisation that brought them together. Later, thanks to a liturgical team formed a long time ago, the Sunday Mass was prepared with songs by the choir. In the hospital there was also Mass prepared by the Sisters, but also by lay people who were called to do the readings. My approach was always to involve as many people as possible. For the recreation in the hospital, every Sunday evening, I showed a film which everyone looked forward to. As for the young boys and girls who were left to their own devices, I had them do colouring, which they then took away with them. A moment of relaxation and freedom where they escaped for a few moments from the drudgery of their lives. Actually, what they said to me to explain their situation was: "We were sent". That meant to go and do all sorts of errands. It ended up weighing on them. At last, a moment to themselves. There were the highlights of the retreat, three days before the baptisms, which were also a moment of grace, including at the camp in Mafou. As the group had some means, they brought a generator. I played a film about Jesus and stayed the night there. For them, this represented a protection, a blessing. The Sisters even came on motorbikes. Once I had to force a major seminarian to come too. He is not likely to forget that lesson. That is what missionary life is all about!

Participation in the meetings of the pastoral sector, as well as in those of the diocese, was something important for me and for the Sisters. This allowed us to be integrated into the diocesan and sectoral pastoral ministry, to get to know the other priests and pastoral agents of the Sector, 15 parishes in the sector and 45 in the diocese, and not to isolate ourselves in our own corner. It was a question of getting to know the people of course, but also the concerns, the sensitivities, the points of view. I also brought my own personal point of view and my way of seeing things, which was very well accepted. Sometimes you don't have to look very far to find a definition of Mission. It's just a matter of being present, of being there, nothing more. The DG (Director General of the IRF), who was a Muslim, told me several times how much he valued the place of a chaplain, of the spiritual, and how reassured and happy he was when he learned that a new Father would come to take up the post of chaplain.

The response of the people.

I have just referred to the reaction of the DG. But the other administrative authorities told me the same thing, as well as some doctors. When one of them lost a 14-year-old son I went to the prayer service. He was from another Church, but he wrote to thank me. A bus accident caused the death of 3 IRF staff, two carers and one administrator. We all met to pray at the hospital church and later to commemorate their birthdays. One was Catholic, one was Buddhist and the other Evangelical. Kouakou, the one who was afraid that I would cut his head off, came to my house to help me carry the equipment for the cinema. The leprosy patients' organisation used to come to my house to have their speeches printed on the day of the leprosy festival: the World Leprosy Day at the end of January. Mutual trust was established. Some of them ran small businesses: selling Soup cubes or phone recharge cards, and they needed change. After Mass they would arrive in their wheelchairs to collect the change from the day's collection. There was not always enough to satisfy them unless I had gone to Mafou where the collection was generally bigger.

The outside world

There were quite a few Muslims who were hospitalised for various reasons. I have recounted elsewhere how one actually came to confess and ask God's forgiveness! At Duquesne-Crmone the imam and the muezzin greeted me regularly. When they were in mourning, I made an offering. The relationship did not go very far. I respected them and I think they respected me. With the Evangelists and other Churches, I practised the same policy of respect. Those who prayed in the hospital asked me for the sound system on certain occasions, which I gladly lent them. But there were no in-depth discussions there either. On the other hand, at one time, a patient came to see me every week to talk with me. I had difficulty identifying who he was. He wanted to initiate me into his traditional religion, he proposed to protect me by mystical or magical practices. How to have power myself. But he ended up asking me for money or other goods as payment. I didn't show much interest in him so he eventually left me alone. To have other meetings outside the hospital or village environment, I would have had to go to Adzopé. I did not meet the administrative, political or police authorities. There was, however, a company manager who did welding, among other things, and whom I asked several times to do some work. He was interesting.

He was a Muslim, and he kept Ramadan. I asked him what that meant to him. I got an answer that I found very beautiful. He told me: "In life we commit a lot of sins and we need time to ask Allah for forgiveness. That's what Ramadan is for, and then you have peace in your heart. God favoured him. He bought my car back and paid me the price I asked for it. What more can I say?

General reflection based on experience

From a personal point of view

I would say that this experience, in this particular, unique environment, has given me a lot. At the IRF I learned a lot about leprosy, Buruli ulcers, and perforating wounds due to diabetes. When the Gospels speak of lepers, it has a different resonance for me now. This led me to ask the Nuncio in the Ivory Coast for a small liturgical reform. I asked him to change the prayer on the Offerings of the Feast of the Transfiguration on August 6, which for me unfortunately says: "Sanctify our offerings, Lord, by the mystery of your Son transfigured in glory; And in the radiance of his light, cleanse us from the leprosy of sin." Why associate leprosy and sin? It is true that leprosy has an extremely negative aura. But it is not due to any sin. The liturgy should not add to the misery of leprosy by making it a paradigm of sin. Let us find something else: ugliness or malice, or simply say: "Cleanse us from sin." It can help to change mentalities, which I feel is important. The IRF hospital started operating in 1950, so it has been 70 years. At the beginning, it was very difficult to recruit personnel. Only the European sisters agreed to touch the lepers to do the dressings. Now, finally, people are prepared to come to work. In 2012, when it was necessary to appoint a new DG, the Minister of Health at the time initially had three refusals. Nobody wanted to go there. In my eyes, the real heroes of the situation are those who provide care. I don't know how to do that, and I have always wanted to stress this point. Even now, when leprosy has decreased a lot and antibiotics are effective, it is still necessary to heal the negative aura that it inevitably arouses.

For someone who is used to loving and caring for those he has been entrusted with, this is not a problem. I have had the opportunity to meet the followers of vodun in Benin, the diamond miners and the pygmies in the Central African Republic. Getting to know the people of the IRF was a different experience of pastoral care, but the method is still the same: to get to know as well as possible the people for whom one is responsible. But it takes time. We would like to go deeper, to identify all the springs that animate people in their way of life. This is the fruit of long -term contact work. Then to transmit to them the values of the Gospel in all the aspects that concern the men and women with whom we are dealing is very delicate. Discernment is needed. You need the inspiration of the Spirit and a lot of empathy, no matter what you think personally.

The African is very religious. For him there is no separation between the profane and the sacred. This is not France. But prayers and blessings don't solve all the problems. The traditional approach to illness and misfortune must evolve. How is this to be done? How can we help people to observe reality as it is and not only see it as invested with a mystical aura? We need to make people aware of where the illness really comes from and to get rid of mythical interpretations. This will take a long time.

For the mission of the Church today

The IRF of the Ivory Coast and the villages related to it appear to me as a privileged place for the Church to exercise its witness of love and service to human beings in distress. This witness can be exercised by ordained ministers such as priests and deacons but also by Religious Sisters and by lay Christians. Jesus' encounter with the lepers in the Gospel is so well known that it is reasonable for us to think that He is always with them, even in 2021. The challenge is to be present not only to the patients but also to the Medical Corps, the carers and the other staff. Some are Catholic, but not all. We have to respect those who are different. But we need to go deeper with those who are Catholic, who come to the exercises of piety, who animate the liturgies of the Mass by singing or doing the readings. We should be able to understand their lives, their activities, their motivations. We should be able to discern the "signs of the times", that is to say, what must evolve and how, the obstacles to be overcome, the line to be taken.

For the SMA mission

I did what I could to inform myself about the history of the IRF. I was able to see how important the commitment of the SMA Fathers and the OLA Sisters in this field of apostolate was. Fr. Miet, Sr. Eugenia and then Frs. Duquesne, Parriaux, Margerit and Arnolfo invested their apostolic efforts in this particular pastoral field. I have tried to continue the furrow marked out by them.

And I hope that the SMA, along with the OLA Sisters, will continue this work, whatever the cost, even if one day leprosy will be eradicated in Ivory Coast. It is exactly the kind of place where the SMA carries out what it holds most dear: to be in the presence of the poor, the wounded in life, the bruised and the rejected. It is certainly in its rightful place. Nevertheless, this does not exclude the fact that the diocesan clergy will also have to take up this ministry one day.

Conclusion

I give thanks to the Lord for having been, if only for a few years, engaged in this task of evangelisation, albeit certainly marked also by many shortcomings. There is so much to do, so much to envision. This is my testimony.

... people with hearing disabilities Ghana

Kouame Rene Dan Yao SMA

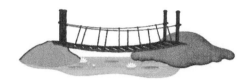

Challenges of people with disabilities

The word "disability" means a physical, sensory, mental, or other impairment, including any visual, hearing, learning or physical incapability, which impacts adversely on social, economic or environmental participation; it is a reality that concerns and touches almost everybody. In one way or another everyone has either an identifiable or hidden disability. It appears obvious that there are various forms of disabilities; some are more serious and some others less. The truth is that all people with visible disabilities suffer from some kinds of injustices either from the society at large or from individuals. Those injustices have created a situation whereby disabled men and women are rejected, so to speak, and given a stigma that prevents them from being fully incorporated into society. They have suffered and continue to endure *discrimination, pain*, and related injustices. So the question is to know how we can help our brothers and sisters today to be **fully** part of our daily activities without any form of *discrimination*. In fact what could each one of us do in order to promote the rehabilitation of disabled people? This article aims at creating a better awareness of what we already know, but we seem to neglect and ignore most of the time. We are called to acknowledge that the challenges of people with disabilities are crucial and cruel; that the social, medical and theological perspective on disability needs to be duly addressed in such a manner as to be able to reach the goal of rehabilitation of people with disabilities into society.

Growing number of people with disabilities

According to an internet source, "More than one billion people in the world live with some form of disability, of whom nearly 200 million experience considerable difficulties in functioning. In the years ahead, disability will be an even greater concern because its prevalence is on the rise. This is due to ageing populations and the higher risk of disability in older people as well as the global increase in chronic health conditions such as diabetes, cardiovascular disease, cancer and mental health disorders." [1]

Across the world, people with disabilities have poorer health outcomes, lower education achievements, less economic participation and higher rates of poverty than people without disabilities. This is partly because people with disabilities experience barriers in accessing services that many of us have long taken for granted, including **health**, **education**, **employment**, and **transport** as well as **information**. These difficulties are exacerbated in less advantaged communities such as the ones in Ghana.

Environmental Challenges

A person's environment has a huge impact on the experience and extent of disability. Inaccessible environments contribute to disability by creating barriers to participation and inclusion. A concrete illustration of the possible negative impact of the environment can be to have *a deaf individual without a sign language interpreter;* for instance in a Parish like Queen of Peace-Madina there was not one service for the deaf in the Church before 29th November 2020. Such an attitude has made a lot of Catholic deaf move to other Churches where at least a service is offered for them. Just as the state needs to provide proper care to improve health conditions, prevent impairments, and improve outcomes for persons with disabilities, we, as human beings in general and particularly as Roman Catholic Christians in the Archdiocese of Accra need by all means to create awareness while working towards the progressive and

---

[1] https://www.unicef.org/protection/World_report_on_disability_eng.pdf

total inclusion of the Deaf People in our midst (liturgically, socially, pastorally, etc). Such changes can be brought about by legislation, policy changes, capacity building, or technological developments leading to, for instance: accessible design of the built environment and transport; signage to benefit people with sensory impairments; more accessible health, rehabilitation, education, and support services; more opportunities for work and employment for persons with disabilities.

A small response to the need

As a response to the above challenges, the Society of African Missions (SMA) Ghana Province allowed the creation of a Ministry fully dedicated to the deaf people in Ghana. By this initiation of the SMA the Roman Catholic Church in Ghana also welcomed the first ever deaf mission apostolate. Launched in the Archdiocese of Accra at the climax of the 140th anniversary of the Society of African Missions (SMA) in Ghana, the St Martin Deaf Ministry spearheaded by *Reverend Father Yao Kouamé René Dan (SMA)* was officially unveiled under the auspices of the Society of African Missions (SMA) at St. Francis of Assisi Parish at Ashaley Botwe, Accra Ghana on Sunday, 22nd of November 2020.

Immediately after being commissioned, the **St Martin Deaf Ministry** started its activities with the first official Mass interpretation into Ghanaian Sign Language (GSL) at Queen of Peace Catholic Church. The activity took place on Sunday, November 29, 2020, during the second mass at 8: 30 am. The St Martin Deaf Ministry was created with a clear VISION to build a foundation for an inclusive community that respects and recognizes humanity rather than the socio-economic and physical status of individuals; the MISSION for its members being to commit themselves to reach out and facilitate the integration process through evangelisation, education, and empowerment; and having as OBJECTIVE to bridge the gap of communication and facilitate the process of integration between the hearing and the deaf community through the usage of Ghanaian Sign Language (GSL) as means of communication.

… people with hearing disabilities USA

Frank Wright SMA

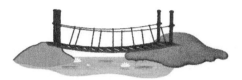

This article is an experiment in the use of the Appreciative Discernment methodology, which we adopted for our last General Assembly. As such, we look at those times in the past, when we have been most truly ourselves, when we have seen our identity and mission work most clearly, and from our reflections, we move ahead to chart a way forward. In many cases, our missionary past comes to us in the form of images that capture something valuable in what we have done and on which we can build.[1]

The Deaf and Disabilities communities

When we talk about going out to the margins of Society, we're really talking about ministry to people who have had the deck stacked against them from the beginning. We're talking about the forgotten and the ignored. In our SMA mission outreach in the past, two such groups that have not received a great deal of attention are the Deaf and Disability communities. … You will notice that I have capitalised (in English) these two groups, because they find themselves shunted to the side-lines and relegated to the role of spectators, even of matters that concern themselves. "Deaf" and "Disabled" are thus no longer adjectives that

---

[1] I will cite only one book in this article. "Memories, Hopes, and Conversations: Appreciative Inquiry, Missional Engagement, and Congregational Change" M. L. BRANSON, Lanham (MD) 2016.

describe a physical condition but rather social descriptors of how people have had their power to make decisions taken away from them. When this happens, one takes away their hope for the future as well. In this sense, they are the abandoned of whom the Founder spoke.

This short reflection on possible paths to the future for SMA missionary outreach is not a foray into systematic theology as such; instead, I'm trying to think from the ground up, working from my own ministry experience as Chaplain for the Department of Special Needs Ministries in the Archdiocese of Washington (DC) and as pastor to the Deaf community in the Washington, DC area.

This reflection is addressed to other members of the SMA family. It is an in-house conversation. There is nothing definitive about it. It is not the last word on the subject; rather, my hope is that it will spark a wide-ranging discussion on how we as SMA approach ministry to persons with various limitations, often termed disabilities. ... What do we have to be aware of? How will it change some of our fundamental and unconscious assumptions about human beings, Society, and Church? How will it enable us to read Scripture more deeply? How shall we ourselves be transformed?

SMA's lack of focus in this area, to which I alluded above, is but a reflection of Society at large. I was talking to a bishop one day, explaining to him that I was working in Deaf ministry. His comment was, "Oh, that's a very specialized ministry." I was taken aback at his reaction, because in an age when every government official who appears on TV has a sign-language interpreter right beside him, it didn't seem to me to be specialized at all.

Nevertheless, his comment was not atypical. As contemporary societies, and even sometimes as Church, we minimize the very existence of people with disabilities: on one hand, we view them as poor unfortunates who must be taken care of (paternalism); and on the other hand, as people not eligible for any accommodations whatsoever. One way or the other, we render them invisible.

What we fail to do is to credit them with being social actors in their own right. Decisions are made for them. Naturally enough, Deaf people and those with disabilities react very negatively to the stigmas and the narratives that the larger society foists upon them; for that reason, the current battle cry from both communities is, "Nothing about us, without us!"

Washington DC and the Deaf Community

In 2013, in the wake of the SMA General Assembly and the installation of a new Provincial Council, I was asked to do a course on ministry to persons with disabilities.[2] I was living in Washington DC at the time and approached the Archdiocese for information. The Department of Special Needs Ministries asked me to work with Blind and Low Vision Catholics on a volunteer basis. After six months, they offered me a full-time position as chaplain to the Deaf community in the DC area, with additional outreach to various Disability communities.[3] Included in my portfolio were working with persons on the Autism Spectrum, Blind and Low-vision people, people with various medical conditions, etc. Unfortunately, since I had no knowledge of American Sign Language at the time, this new endeavour represented a very steep learning curve for me.[4]

Let me tell you something about the Catholic, Deaf community in Washington DC. What are they like? Well, as a community, they prefer using American Sign Language and will take advantage of interpreting services, whenever they are made available. ... The vast majority of Deaf persons in the US marry other Deaf people. ... In some cases, there is a long tradition of deafness in families; one lady whom I know is the fifth generation in her family to be Deaf: however, this is not typical, as most persons who are Deaf are born into hearing families. ... The parishioners at St. Francis Deaf Catholic Church in Landover Hills, Maryland are mostly university-educated, working in a wide variety of jobs, particularly in the field of accounting; in fact, the Federal government is active in recruiting Deaf persons for this kind of work. As a community, they are very tight-knit and move as much as possible in the Deaf world.

---

[2] This was surprising, because I normally work with communities that are linguistic minorities. I suppose the Provincial Council thought that since I am a person with severe visual disabilities and increasing hearing loss, this would be right up my alley.

[3] You will notice that I have capitalised in English various terms describing what are normally considered to be physical attributes; however, since these are in many cases social descriptors, I have followed the usage of writers in this field and capitalised them.

[4] I remained in that position for four years. Although I attained a reasonable fluency in using ASL, my ability to follow conversations was below par. Having reached an age to go on senior status, I opted to make way for a Deaf priest from Korea who was fluent in ASL.

From my years with the community, there are various images that stick in my mind, images that can serve as a foundation for further reflection. For example, after our Sunday morning mass at St. Francis Deaf Catholic Church, the entire community of perhaps fifty people would move upstairs for lunch and remain until 3 PM. On occasion, there would be a program, or a community meeting, but in most cases, people just remained at their tables, conversing and eating.

In the dining room, they enjoy being able to use sign language, in a venue where it is not only easily understood but the norm. They have common experiences of the world: in many cases they attended the same boarding institutions for their education. Most are graduates of Gallaudet University (the only university in the world exclusively for Deaf people.) They have the same horror stories of dealing with a hearing bureaucracy, whether in government offices, hospitals, or the legal system. At the church, they are in a safe space, as opposed to the outside world, where they are always at a disadvantage. They are people who enjoy being with each other, and the existence of a Deaf community is of paramount importance for them.

A second image that remains with me is that of the Easter Vigil at the church.[5] American Sign Language is a very expressive language, and when in the hands of a consummate signer, it can be truly uplifting. We were fortunate in having among our parishioners several former members from the National Theatre for the Deaf, and when they undertook to sign the Exultet, you could see the stars and the angels in the heavens. In the first reading from Genesis, you could see the birds and all crawling creatures come alive. Deaf culture possesses a richness that is normally invisible to the world at large.

More images: Washington DC and its environs has several l'Arche homes for adults with disabilities. There also exists Bethlehem House near Catholic University, which was independently founded by Dolores Wilson. On Wednesday evenings, a group of priests, including myself, took turns celebrating mass for the residents and for a group of students from the University. After mass, the residents and visitors would sit down for a meal. Each resident in the house had a counterpart "best buddy" from Catholic University, who would bond with the resident during that school year. This experience was a fine example of

---

[5] We did not follow the rubric of starting the vigil in the darkness of the night because people need to 'see' the signs of the priest outside the Church.

collaboration between persons with no discernible disability (the students) and those who live in a residential institution.

More images: every other year, the Department of Special Needs Ministries, for which I worked, would host a conference on Faith and Deafness and Disability. This generally took place on a weekend at a Catholic High School and gathered some five hundred people together to attend workshops. The sessions were sometimes about how to access services available from the government or other service organisations, and sometimes they were organised in order to make people aware that they are not alone.

Both Fr. Austin Ochu SMA and I have given workshops on the international face of disabilities. In an urban area with a strong immigrant presence from Latin America and Africa, these workshops tried to bridge the gap between the experiences of what it means to be disabled in people's home countries and what they encountered in the US.[6] The immigrant experience is very often an isolating one. People lack familiarity with the labyrinth of government structures and services. They often lack an opportunity to reflect on how attitudes towards persons with disabilities might be different.

A final image: The Archdiocese of Washington, under the leadership of Cardinal Donald Wuerl, initiated the establishment of local entities entitled Community Resource groups. Although possessing a strong Catholic connection, these groups were in fact non-denominational and non-religious organisations. These small groups provided recreational resources for persons with disabilities, both children and adults, as well as opportunities for the dissemination of vital information. They represent a good example of collaboration between different faith-based groups and other service organisations.

There are other images that I could bring up, such as the White Mass, so called because everyone was asked to wear white clothing. This was celebrated by the Cardinal in St. Matthew's Cathedral to raise awareness of the needs of persons with disabilities. Or I could mention the Easter Vigil, organised by Bethlehem House for the Faith and Light Community (a worldwide group founded by Hélène Matthieu in France). In this celebration, the events of Holy Week were telescoped into one afternoon to provide a connected narrative that persons with disabilities could follow. But enough examples! I am sure that each of us could provide our own.

---

[6] Workshops were offered in English and Spanish.

What can we take away from these images? The first point is that we must approach this ministry in a spirit of humility, and perhaps of wonder. As mentioned before, I experienced a steep learning curve in familiarizing myself with American Sign Language and with the field of disability studies. There is a lot to be learned from the people with whom we work. People in the Deaf and Disability communities possess a rich culture, and it takes time to appreciate it.

In many cases, the strength of the Department of Special Needs Ministries lay in making sure that information was available to people so that they could access assistance at various levels. All these efforts were part and parcel of empowering people to become social actors in their own right. We are not starting from ground zero in doing this. There is already a fine tradition of people speaking up for themselves.[7] At the present time, the Coordinator for Deaf Ministry in DC is herself Deaf, a position to which she brings her extensive education as a social worker. We as ministers do not have to speak for them, but we do have to make sure that they have a chance to be heard.

One of our strengths of the Department has been that of collaboration, both with service organisations, with other faith-based groups, and with lay people.[8] There is work that people who are not priests can do better than priests. There is nothing astounding about what I am saying here. People from all walks of life possess talents in teaching, in administration, in networking, in organisation, and in inspiring people through example. We are all in the business of hope.

In our approach, we must not underestimate the importance of community on two levels: first, persons with disabilities are strengthened, when they can join together with people who have common experiences of oppression. There is strength in numbers, and the existence of a community with common experiences provides an opportunity for persons with disabilities to appropriate who they are on many levels.

---

[7] I had the privilege of seeing/hearing Greg Hilbok, now an attorney, who was one of the leaders of the rebellion by students at Gallaudet University back in 1988, forcing the Board of Governors to finally select a Deaf Person as president of the University.

[8] I would be remiss if I did not mention the fine work at Hope for Life, a community for persons with mobility issues in Accra. This project was founded by Fr. Jean Thébault of the Lyons Province and some local persons with disabilities who were tired of begging on the streets. Various lay associates from the US, the Netherlands, and France collaborated in this work.

In addition, community on the level of Church and Society is important, because we need to make sure that persons with disabilities find their rightful place in the larger Church community. In liturgy, this may mean encouraging them to fulfil roles as lectors, acolytes, and have the chance to try their vocations as religious and priests.[9]

The Western and African Contexts

In the United States, and I would assume in Europe as well, having a disability is regarded as unsightly. In the U.S., when we were young, we were admonished by our mothers not to look at a person on crutches, or someone with a seeing-eye dog, or at anybody missing a limb. The message was very clear: don't call attention to them. Their existence is embarrassing. Those with disabilities occupied an ambiguous space in the public sphere, where they weren't to be seen, and if they were, they were to be objects of pity. There was something wrong with them physically that didn't fit in with the men and women that we were meant to be, meant to be particularly in all the images of human perfection in the media.

This stigma and narratives that we foist on persons with disabilities has its darker side. When I was working with the Department of Special Needs Ministries, I had the pleasure of working professionally with the mother of a daughter who had had various disabilities due to a broken gene, and for that reason, she was deaf, mostly blind, with limited cognitive ability. One time, when my co-worker was organizing a group home for adults like her daughter, one of the attendees at the meeting, who was opposed to having the group home in her neighbourhood, asked what was wrong with these people. Why were they abnormal? Were they the children of parents who took drugs? Having a disability can appear like having a moral failing. You're not perfect on several levels.[10]

---

[9] There are at present ten Deaf priests in the United States, working in various capacities, many with the Deaf communities in their dioceses.
[10] Disability is viewed as imperfection. Often the question comes, if you had a chance to not have a disability, would you avail yourself of the change? I have severe limitations to my eyesight and am what we term in the US as a person with low vision. My answer, and that of many other people with limitations is that I don't think so. I have never known anything different. The issue rears its head in the discussion of persons on the Autism Spectrum. Is our concern,

This ambiguity is enshrined in literature. One of my favourite books is Charles Dickens' "The Christmas Carol." Tiny Tim, crippled and with a persistent cough that looks suspiciously like tuberculosis, has his place by the fire, where he can hang up his crutch. There he sits, unless he is being trotted out as an object for our compassion. Although apprenticeships are being sought for his brother Peter, Tiny Tim will be lucky if he can sell matches by the side of the road.

I think the role of persons with disabilities is just as ambiguous in the African context, but perhaps for different reasons. They have their allotted space both in the family circle and in the larger society; however, one big difference is that they are not invisible. They are not freaks of nature the way that they can be viewed in Western culture. African society has a tighter grip on reality than what I see in the West. From what I have seen in the cities and in the villages, they are accepted as members of the family because of the strong family system. They are taken care of and enjoy more freedom to roam around than would be accorded them in the US. [11]

In regard to our carrying out ministry, these different ways of being ambiguous may be to our advantage in the African context. Since the existence of persons with disabilities is a fact of life in African societies, we at least don't have to take them out of hiding. I grant you that we may have many other battles to fight: Deaf people and those with disabilities are just as much shunted to the side-lines in Africa as they are in the West, but in my experience, they are just as insistent on being heard as they are elsewhere. As bearers of the Gospel, our efforts may entail standing in solidarity with persons with disabilities, as they strive to avail themselves of the common resources that belong to everyone in Society; however, our concern is also to ensure that persons with disabilities can be seen as integral of who we are.

A nice example of what I'm talking about took place at the canonisation of St. Junipero Serra in Washington DC back in 2015. The second reading was proclaimed by a young lady with Down Syndrome. One of the Prayers of the Faithful was signed and voiced by a former actor of the National Theatre for the Deaf (and my parishioner.) The point is not tokenism, making sure that we have a representative from

---

particularly as Church, to cure Autism, or to make sure that people with Autism can be social actors in their own right?

[11] My experience encompasses Chad in the 1970s, Northern Nigeria in the 1980s, Ivory Coast in the early 1990's, and Kenya in the 1990's and 2000's.

all the different segments in the community; rather, the point is to form a community, where all believers are seen as emblematic of the Body of Christ. Not tolerance; not inclusion; rather belonging. We're all here; we're all together!

By way of a conclusion

The Appreciative Discernment methodology doesn't lead to conclusions in the same way that other deliberative methodologies do. If there is one idea that characterizes the outcome of our discussions, it is that we are alive to the many possibilities that may be present in any situation. Furthermore, the methodology does not embrace a top-down flow of ideas and results. Inspiration may come at any level. To phrase it differently: one grand scheme does not fit all situations.

What I have offered are images and an interpretation of those images. In short, something occurs in life, and we recognize that something as significant, as something authentic, and as something true to our charism as SMA. At that point, we try to flesh out what has happened and why it is important. From the images and the accompanying reflections, take what you can. The genius of Appreciative Discernment is that it can generate new ideas at many levels. What should remain constant in any endeavour is the desire to halt practices of paternalism (Father knows best) and give Deaf people and persons with disabilities a place at the table, a place at the ambo, and a place in the evangelizing mission of the Church.

... people in the mission field Tanzania

Mariel Sumallo SMA

The Lord has spoken through our Mother Church to remind us that we are brothers and sisters—we are together!

The Encyclical of Pope Francis, *Fratelli Tutti* is indeed a gift to humanity and to the whole of creation which helps us on our journey to encounter the Lord together as brothers and sisters.

When our unity as children of God seems threatened and neglected, it is a consolation to know that there are people who strive to protect and value that unity. Some of them live in mud houses, some cannot even write their names, while others have never even seen a television. But visit them and they will be very happy to see you, and they will cook meat, rice and beans for you, and I can tell you, "Tuko Pamoja," we are together.

Fratelli Tutti. Tuko Pamoja. We are brothers and sisters. We are together.

Into the Sukuma land

Mary Mother of God Parish of Bugisi is located in the Diocese of Shinyanga, Tanzania, East Africa. The parish was established by the Maryknoll Fathers in 1959 and was handed over to the Society of African Missions (SMA) in 1990. It is composed of 34 outstations in the heart of

147

the Sukuma land. This is a place where we patiently waited for rain for almost 8 months this year 2021.

Our parishioners love being together. They can spend the day sharing food and stories together, and they seem to have a natural gift for storytelling and patience for listening. I never failed to notice that, whenever I go to an outstation, I always find them gathered under a tree or beside the chapel enjoying a lively conversation while waiting for the priest. Then after Mass, they always find time to talk and to wish everyone a good day. Their unity as a community is what brings life to the church and to the society. Everyone is cared for and looked after. Their houses may be miles apart, but distance has not been a barrier, for them to be brothers and sisters.

Others' preconceived ideas

Their culture however has not been spared from biased criticisms. Their love of being together is sometimes labelled as "waste of time" or "laziness."

Contrary to those labels, they are hardworking people. In fact, they can work so hard that the fruit of their labour is enough to support the Church and to feed their families the entire year. The rain has been scarce for the past 7 months now, and yet they still have enough food on their plates.

Sometimes their culture is compared very negatively with other cultures. Is it even fair to compare one culture with another? Phrases like "At home we don't do that" or "The way they do things, it's just not acceptable in my country" or "They need to change the way they do things" are common remarks I hear from strangers—even from missionaries! How much do we know about them? I believe that, unless we learn to accept the fact that they are part of who we are, we will never fully appreciate their culture and the beauty of their being. They have much to share; we just have to open our hearts.

Social implications of the ideas

One day I went to a small village for a funeral Mass. I thought to myself "There will be nothing special about it, it's just a small village anyway." But when I got to the village, I was stunned to see hundreds of people mourning with the family: Muslims, Evangelicals, Baptists, Catholics and traditionalists. They were all together. Even our Muslims brothers helped lay the body of our Catholic faithful into her final resting place.

148

Many of them travelled from far places: some by cars, others by bicycles and or by foot. Regardless of their differences in beliefs and status in life, they were united as a community to be with the family in need.

In his Encyclical Pope Francis pointed out that in some places people are neighbours, but they don't treat each other as brothers and sisters. But here they are actually not neighbours by proximity yet they are still brothers and sisters and are one.

They are together in times of planting, harvesting and plenty and are still together in times of grief, scarcity, and in times of drought. They are together in times of celebration, in times of joy. *Fratelli Tutti: Tuko Pamoja*. We are brothers and sisters. We are together.

Let's get dusty

We are called to be with the people. We don't only smell like our sheep; we also get dusty to be with them. A missionary should never be afraid to get dusty to get to the outstations or small Christian communities *(jumuia)* even those that are in the middle of the bush. People often laugh when they hear me say, "If you cannot find the road, make one." But it's true. I literally make my own road just to get to the people. If we want to get connected with others, we must find ways or make roads and bridges just to get closer to them.

Once there was a visitor who was insistent on accompanying us to the villages. One day we invited him for Sunday Mass in the outstation. We had Mass and talked to the people and then we visited five sick people and gave them Holy Communion, visited a family in the middle of a farm and went to another village to attend the memorial celebration of one of our catechists who had died. The sun was hot and the roads were bad and dusty. By the time we got back to the house, it was already dark. We got home tired and hungry. He saw and experienced our ministry—it was tough. Since then he has never asked again to join us at the outstation.

As missionaries, how could we carry out our ministry without being with the people? We could use different strategies in the hope of making our ministry effective. But at the end of the day it's the quality of an encounter that will leave a mark upon the hearts of the people, and hopefully, bring them closer to God. It doesn't worry me if they forget our homilies, but at least, they will say "Father remembered us. He came to our house even if the road was bad."

Pastoral initiative

Central to the charism of the Society of African Missions is the evangelisation of the peoples. especially the most abandoned in Africa. And the SMA has been faithful to that call since it's foundation in 1856. The Church never lacks pastoral strategies. In fact, there are so many of them that sometimes it's hard to choose which one would be effective in a particular pastoral situation. And for me as a new missionary who is still learning the local language of the people, evangelisation through words can be a challenge. Nevertheless, this does not stop me from carrying out my ministry even if I have to be creative in order to do so.

The parish of *Bugisi* and its outstations are already well established. Everyone knows what to do and how to do them in order to give life and to sustain the parish and chapels. There are spiritual talks, seminars, Adoration, Rosary and other faith-related activities. But one of the elements of pastoral work that I find vital for the success of our ministry is the quality of our **Ministry of Presence.**

Quality Presence is defined as the ability to project a sense of ease, poise, or self-assurance, especially the quality or manner of a person's bearing before an audience. But here in the mission, quality presence means praying with the people, celebrating with them, dancing with them, sharing food with them, not rushing to get home after an activity is done, enjoying quality conversation with them or patiently listening to their stories. The quality of our ministry of presence is going to be the most important aspect of our mission here in Africa as SMA missionaries.

Response of the people

Baba, tuko pamoja! "Father, we are together". This is the response of the people when they also feel that their priest is one with them.

Is it easy to maintain quality presence whenever we are ministering to the people? The simple answer is "No." It's not easy. It's not easy when I'm sleepy and tired. It's not easy when my mind is occupied with all the other things to do when I get back to the parish house. It's not easy when it's humid and I'm exhausted because of the long journey. Hundreds of reasons can surface that can compromise the quality of our ministry of presence. Nevertheless, when the quality of our Ministry of Presence is maintained in our pastoral activities, the following are some of the wonderful effects upon the faithful:

The relationship with God is nourished.

Our faithful are aware that it is God who called us to be missionaries. And when they feel that their priests are close to them, they also feel that God is close to them. I always remember one particular visit to one of our outstations. An elderly woman came dancing and singing with her hands raised and thanking God for having remembered them through the presence of His priests.

When people feel that Padre wants to spend quality time with them, people come for confession and open themselves to the loving mercy of God. With their hearts and minds renewed, they can approach God with open hands and they glorify God wholeheartedly. It is very touching to see them singing and dancing during Mass. The people know and can feel if the time their priests share with them is meant for them to be together. If they do feel that, then that time becomes sacred for them and becomes a cause for a wonderful celebration.

The joy and blessings that people receive through the quality of our ministry of presence encourages others to come to Church. Parents bring their children to Church. Our faithful invite neighbours to come for Mass and prayers. It gladdens the hearts of missionaries to see the Church filled with people who are dancing, singing and praising God with their whole hearts.

The relationship with the Church is strengthened.

The quality of our Ministry of Presence strengthens the unity of the people and, in effect, it encourages them to support the Church.

During the village Masses of Thanksgiving for the harvests, people offer their support to the church through the fruits of their labour. They offer rice, beans, vegetables, peanuts, eggs, fruits and many other products. They are that generous because they know that the Church is theirs. They feel responsible for it and are willing to take care of it. That is why they maintain their chapels and clean them even if the chapel is just made of simple mud bricks dug out of the ant hills. It is touching to see how they decorate their chapels even if the bricks are already in a poor state because of the rain.

Many of our parishioners are poor but regardless of their situation, they are always there for the Church. They may not have a coin to offer during Mass, but their presence is what is most pleasing to God especially when it has taken them more than an hour's walk under the scorching sun to get to the church. Sometimes the collection during Sunday Mass in some of the outstations is only two dollars. We know it's not much; however we also know that that's the best they could offer. I always get emotional every time I touch an old and tattered 1, 000 shillings (50cents) because I know it means a fortune to them. But out of love for the Church they untie the coins they have from the folded edge of their clothes and offer them to God. They are willing to share what they have because they know that we are one, and therefore we are responsible for each other and also for our Church.

The relationship with our brothers and sisters is deepened.

One of our parishioners said, "Father, we look up to our priests because they are our leaders and spiritual fathers." It sounds unimportant and simple but if we look deeply into it, it speaks so much as to what a society could be like. When they see and feel that priests are willing and capable of really living out the ministry of presence, they imitate it and it becomes a prevailing culture in the church.

We should not worry much that some don't remember our homilies, but we should be very aware that they are observing us. They are trying to figure out how to live their Christian lives by observing and imitating how their leaders live their Christian lives.

Their generosity of presence whenever someone is in need tells much about the depth of their affection and sense of responsibility towards each other. Young and old, men and women, pagans or believers, they are all together in times of plenty and scarcity, in times of grief or in times of joy. They have no walls that divide them. Even the miles of distance that separate them do not stop them from being connected with others.

Their freedom from fear of intimacy and encounter makes the church alive and vibrant. People can dance, sing and talk with each other because they are not hindered by the culture of walls. They can eat from one plate. They can sit together under the shade of a mango tree. They can take care of each others' children. They can drink from the same cup. These simple acts forge their relationship into something stronger, and it allows them to feel and embrace everyone as brothers and sisters. And one of the most rewarding aspects of being in the mission is the experience of being loved not for what we can do, but for who we are.

Response of the wider world

One day I was talking to one of our lay missionaries from the United States. She said that she had learned a lot of wonderful things from the people in the parish. And I believe her response was an encapsulation of the response of the wider world, a profound response to an encounter of renewal.

Feel Life: Her life in the US and in Europe was centred upon "getting things done." Work. Work. Work. Everything had to be done right way. Things had to be fast and instant. And she got used to it. But when she immersed herself in the mission she was challenged to slow down and to feel not just others but also herself, which was something counter-cultural for her.

Indeed, the deep rooted culture of the people provides for an authentic encounter which challenges us to slowdown. It challenges us to stop. It challenges us to look. It challenges us to feel and listen. It may sound counter-cultural for many cultures that are evolving too quickly, but that culture is what makes the people flourish in harmony with each other and with nature. Because of that encounter with the people, she discovered her passion for gardening and doing handicrafts. She went back to the US happy about the things she had discovered and feeling grateful for having learned how to cherish life more.

Share: "Give me something," was a statement that made her feel uneasy. Having grown up in a culture that has succumbed to individualism, sharing was something challenging. Her response to such a plea was, "Why would I give you something?"

Is it possible to give without receiving something in return? For the people of our parish, it is possible. The time she spent with the people made her appreciate the culture of sharing. It was a touching experience for her when, every time she visited her friends, they welcomed her into their houses as part of the family and even prepared food for her. Those encounters made her feel loved and welcomed. She realised that sharing is not just all about what we can get or what we can give. Sharing is all about acceptance. When we give, we share our selves. When we receive, we accept the other. The culture of sharing brings us together. It allows us to welcome others into our lives.

Unity: To add my own story, one day we harvested rice with our altar servers. My plan was simple: I just wanted everything done in one day. I organised the altar servers into two groups and stationed them one meter apart from each other. I did it intentionally so that they would avoid talking and focus more on finishing the work. After ten minutes they were all on one side of the rice paddy having a lively conversation while doing their work. What I failed to understand was that for them it was not just about the work, but it was also about intimacy—a renewed encounter. This encounter challenged me to widen my understanding. There is more to life than getting things done.

Many things could be said on the subject. But what was striking for me was the reaction of our friends from other countries about those stories. They were astonished when they heard them. Many of them could not even believe how differently they do things here. As much as they were fascinated by them, they were also saddened by the reality that, in many countries, people are losing the very fabric of our culture that brings us together as brothers and sisters. They felt challenged to renew and protect our culture of unity as children of God.

Reflection: An encounter

The theme of our Come-and-See program in the Philippines when I joined the SMA in 2010 was "Go, then to all nations and make them my disciples: baptize them in the name of the Father, the Son, and the Holy Spirit, and teach them to obey everything I have commanded you. And I will be with you always, to the end of the ages."

That promise of the Lord that He will be with us until the end of the ages makes me think that the message of the Encyclical is one of those encounters with the Lord who promised to be with us always. An authentic encounter with the Lord is always life-changing. It always helps us see things as they are and not as we want them to be.

From a personal point of view

The Encyclical of Pope Francis, *Fratelli Tutti*, speaks about the core of my missionary vocation as an SMA priest. Have I not been called to be with my brothers and sisters? Have I not been called to be one with them? Have I not been called to be the channel of God's peace, to bring about unity and love? When the world is being tempted to succumb to the emerging culture of consumerism and the culture of walls, the Lord has reminded us through the Church what should be the centre of our lives: God and people.

The encyclical challenges me to renew my encounter with the Lord and with the people. I am grateful that I have come to know the people of our parish whose culture and way of life has taught me to value and appreciate the people and events that have shaped my life.

From the mission of the Church today

The documents of Vatican II *Gaudium et Spes and Ad Gentes* affirm the faithfulness of the Church to her mission to bring Christ to the world, the light of humanity, for the salvation of humankind. The Church is a home for encounter. We encounter God in the Church. We encounter the people in the Church. The church is there to help us feel God, our brothers and sisters, ourselves and nature. But do we still see the Church in that way?

We may be fascinated by the content of the Encyclical, but let's not forget where it is from. It is from the Catholic Church. This means that the Church continues to express its love and concern for humanity and the whole of creation. The Encyclical is a profound expression of its care for us all because it can serve as our guide towards that Renewed Encounter with our brothers and sisters. The Encyclical is of great help to us, to forge our unity as one family of the Lord.

What is the use of having great structures in parishes if our unity as brothers and sisters is compromised? What is the use of having sophisticated pastoral strategies if we cannot even profess the fact that we are brothers and sisters? Just as the apostles were told by the Lord to go back to Galilee that their faith and lives may be renewed, so the Lord is reminding us through the Encyclical to go back to who we were created to be, and with St. Francis of Assisi we dare to say, "We are brothers and sisters."

The Diocese of Shinyanga has always promoted and supported the culture of unity and brotherhood of the people. It is visible during diocesan gatherings that we SMA missionaries have attended. All priests are present and all religious communities are represented. The countless people gathered to celebrate with the religious and clergies are also a testimony of the unity the local Church has forged with the people.

From the mission of the SMA

In his book, *"Like the Apostles,"* Fr. Bruno *Semplicio* SMA reminds us that, in his life, Mgr de *Bresillac* considered himself as a man called by God and as an instrument for his glory in the world. Therefore, he acted, he spoke, he suffered and engaged himself to the best of his ability, never self-centred, readily disposed to let everything go, even his life, if that were necessary. Because he felt called, he sought to know what he should do and used all necessary means to discern Our Lord's will." Just like our founder, we must unconditionally plunge ourselves to do the will of God "from the bottom of our hearts."

The grace of God is always there to help us in our missionary work. But let's not forget that the success of our ministry depends upon the unity of the people. Thus, we must do everything to protect and value the culture of the people which encourages us to have a renewed encounter with God and with our brothers and sisters. And before we even think of ourselves as missionaries, let us first remember that we are children of God and we are brothers and sisters.

Just as Jesus and the Father are one, so must we bring about oneness among the people. We are brothers and sisters, we are one. Our Founder reminded us in the *Retreat to Missionaries* that, "It is necessary that we be in the work of God, that we be completely in that work, immersed in it, identified with it, engulfed in its accomplishment; it is essential that this work be our life, our raison d'être." [1]

One concrete example of the responses of the SMA to the plea of humanity is the work of Fr. Patrick Devine, SMA at the Shalom Centre for Conflict Resolution and Reconciliation. This centre works to end the cycle of violence in the tribal lands of Eastern Africa and is a profound response to that challenge to love and care the good of humanity. And also the SMA project for albino children initiated by Fr. Janusz Machota, SMA with the Loretto Sisters in Tanzania, East Africa offers hope and life for many children who are not just neglected but also in fear of abuse.

The Society of African Missions is a channel of unity. Together with the Church, the Society also proclaims that we are brothers and sister: "*Fratelli Tutti!*" And it also proclaims that we are together, "*Tuko Pamoja!*"

---

[1] MELCHIOR DE MARION BRESILLAC, *Retreat to Missionaries*, Rome 1991, 39

... people emerging from long wars Angola

Yakubu Sabo Salisu SMA

Nambuangongo is a Município (Local Government Area) situated in the Province of Bengo in northern part of Angola. It has six *comunas* (townships) and seventy-three *aldeias* (villages). Geographically speaking, it covers 5, 653km2. As of 2014, it had a population of 61, 024 people.[1] The majority of the people who live in this region are Kimbundo by tribe and also speak the Kimbundo language. The other two minority tribes in the region are the Bacongo who speak the Kicongo language, and then the Mbundo who speak the Mbundo language.

In the whole of this vast area, there is only one parish – Nossa Senhora da Assunção, Nambuangongo. It has 29 outstations. In this article, I do not intend to give a scholarly discourse on mission, but rather to share my limited experience of working among a particular set of people with their history as they narrated it to me. I shall give a more detailed background of the area that led to the challenges we are facing now. Then I shall try to give an insight into our mission and how the people are responding to it. Finally, I will conclude with a theological reflection.

---

[1] https://pt.m.wikipedia.org/wiki/Nambuangongo

Background to the present reality – The two wars in Angola

Angola is a country that is still recovering from the wounds of war. The first war – Luta de Libertação de Angola – began in 1961 and ended in 1975 with the celebration of independence. This is the war fought between Angolans and the colonial masters (Portuguese) in order to gain independence. During this war, many missionaries were expelled from the country because the indigenous people identified them with the colonial masters. This affected in a special way the Catholic Church in Nambuangongo since at that time, all the priests working in this area were foreigners. They all left and the people were scattered all over without any spiritual assistance. Other denominations, like the Methodists, benefitted from this since many of their pastors were already Angolans. Some of my older parishioners told me how it was difficult for one to identify oneself as Catholic during this time. Many of them left for the Methodist church for lack of a leader or guide. Others left because they were afraid they might also be killed since their Church had been identified with the colonial masters.

The second war – Guerra Civil – began in 1975 and ended in 2002.[2] This is the war that was fought between the two major rebel movements: the People's Movement for the Liberation of Angola (MPLA) and the National Union for the Total Independence of Angola (UNITA). These two and other minor movements were united in the revolt against the colonial masters. Unfortunately, almost immediately after independence, they began to fight among themselves because each one wanted to be in power. MPLA was in power at the time of Independence but was fiercely resisted by UNITA.

MPLA had its strongholds in Luanda and other cities while UNITA was mainly in control of the rural areas. Since Nambuangongo was a vast rural area sharing the border with Congo DRC from where large quantities of weapons entered the country in order to support UNITA, it became more or less a battle ground during the war. Many young men and women were forced to join the rebel movement and take up arms against the MPLA government – today they are called *anitigo combatentes* (old combatants) and they receive monthly salaries from the

---

[2]

https://pt.m.wikipedia.org/wiki/Guerra_de_Independ%C3%AAncia_de_Angol
a

government. Some of my catechists told me how they went to Congo DRC in order to collect arms and ammunitions.

Effects of the wars on the people of Nambuangongo

On this point, I am focusing in particular on Nambuangongo because during the war, Luanda and other cities were not so much affected since the government was fully in control of those areas. As in every war, many lives were lost; women suffered sexual abuse at the hands of soldiers and rebels; many women were widowed and children orphaned; many houses, churches and other institutions were destroyed; and countless number of people fled into the bush for refuge. There, they were scattered on the tops of mountains and hills for many years. Others, including women, went to Congo DRC as refugees and lived there for many years until the end of the war. Lack of spiritual accompaniment for these people, and most especially for the Catholic members, made many lose hope and even today they do not identify with any church or religion, not even the African traditional religion. Consequently, they also admit that they have lost their cultural values as well.

Secondly, where there is no peace there cannot be any meaningful development in the areas of social amenities. For this reason, Nambuangongo was left without water, roads, electricity, healthcare facilities, education, etc. Right up to the present the mortality rate, especially for children, is very high. People travel long distances on foot in order have access to medical facilities and in some cases children die along the road before getting to the hospital. In terms of education, there are primary schools at the centres of the *comunas* with a secondary school at the centre of the *município*. This means that in this vast area (5, 653km2) there are only six primary schools and one secondary school. How can these sufficiently serve the seventy-three *aldeias* of the *município*? On top of this, the schools are not effective because teachers are not always there to teach. Perhaps I also need to make a short comment on the situation of the roads. There is only one tarred road in the whole of Nambuangongo, and this is the road that connects to a junction (Onzo) which leads to all the various *aldeias* of Nambuangongo. Most of the other roads are not suitable for vehicles, and this makes transportation very difficult for people especially during the rainy season. Hence a lot of agricultural products get spoiled on the farm. For a people who depend on agriculture for their subsistence, this means poverty.

Another effect of the war I would like to mention is the fact that it has led to a life of individualism among our people. War might not be the only cause of this problem, but I believe it has contributed a lot to it. When the people came back from the bush and the neighbouring countries to which they had fled for refuge, many chose to settle in isolated areas. Some settled there because that is where they found some land to cultivate while others simply prefer to be all by themselves. Therefore, there are many villages now which are far distant from others. There seems to be suspicion and mistrust also among those who live together in the same village. Added to this is also the belief in witchcraft as a result of which many blame their siblings or neighbours for almost every misfortune be it death, sickness or accident. The solution to this for such people is to visit *kimbandeiros* (native doctors) who then worsen the situation. Consequently, bringing people together to form a Church community, an association or any kind of group with a common interest, is very difficult. Many are indifferent to political activities in the area. Many no longer go to Church and do not subscribe to any religion for that matter. And the fact that the parish for about four years had no parish priest or resident priest led to the closure of four outstations and in many others, many people abandoned the Church. As I write this now, my parishioners in all the twenty-nine outstations are not more than five hundred people.

Our mission

Our mission is to preach the Christian faith; restore trust and confidence among people; and to promote their social well being. We try to do this in various ways.

Prayers and masses

The greatest and most important work of a priest is prayer. Therefore, as people of faith, we pray constantly with and for our people for both spiritual and socio-political and economic transformation of the area. And so as in every other parish, we celebrate Mass on Sundays and other days of the week at the parish centre while other nearby communities have their days of Masses within the week. Here at the centre, we usually pray the rosary every day before Mass and then integrate the breviary into the Mass. In the outstations we encourage people to always pray the rosary before they begin the Celebration of the Word. We find strength in the fact that a few people are responding positively to this.

In our homilies, we try to point out some practices among the people which are not in line with Gospel values. Abuse of alcohol, drugs and sex is widespread in our area. Perhaps this is the reason why there are many cases of unplanned pregnancies and children being abandoned by their parents, especially the fathers. Another major area which we are still trying hard to correct has to do with funerals and the impression that every misfortune is caused by witchcraft. For instance when a man dies, the widow or widows must sleep with his corpse naked in front of everyone around. These and some other practices we put in both our personal and community prayers asking God for healing.

Formation of catechists

Catechists are like priests in their communities. They lead Sunday celebration of the Word, lead funeral celebrations, teach catechism where there are candidates and prepare the people for the visit of the priest. They are the community leaders in everything that pertains to faith and morals. They are the first to be approached whenever there is a problem. However many of them did not receive a sufficient formation. This is the main reason why our mission is difficult. So we organize retreats and seminars for them from time to time, especially during the dry season. They usually come and spend some days at the parish centre during the time of formation. We invite some other priests or catechists to help us facilitate these programs, and in some cases, we do it ourselves. The programs usually cover topics that have to do with the Bible, Catechism, Sacraments, family and health. Our plan now is to train new catechists who will serve as auxiliaries and later successors to the present ones given that many of them are old and sick. But the challenge here is that we do not have young people who are willing to be catechists. In fact, many young people do not even go to Church.

Education and enlightenment

We have already noted above that there is a serious problem in the area of education. While we recognize the efforts of the government in building a few schools in the *município*, we must admit that this is not enough. Therefore, as a Church we try to supplement the efforts of the government. For now, we have a nursery school (São Martinho de Pores) at the Parish Centre, Gombe, which is being taken care of again by the Sisters. We have forty children registered. The aim of this is to help parents, especially mothers, go to farm and do their work freely. They bring their children to school which is in the Church premises. The Sisters teach them some basic literacy and support them in areas of maternal care and nutrition.

This helps them to have a solid educational background. We also have a plan to build a school, and by the grace of God, we will accomplish this plan. We have already got a plot of land big enough to build a school and even a church in the future.

The major challenge here is that the parents of these children are not willing to contribute anything for the good of their children. We have tried different methods of contribution (money or farm produce), but none is working. We rely completely on the help we get from friends and benefactors. Worse is that some parents do not even send their children at the right time when they could learn some lessons. They bring them only when it is time for lunch so that they could just eat and go back home. We have tried to correct this, but so far only a little progress has been made. We are now trying to register the school with the government to see if we could get some help from them. We have done all that is required of us by the government, and are now just awaiting their response.

Healthcare

As missionaries, we try our level best to give special attention to the sick and elderly. Thanks to God, my predecessor built a clinic – *Centro de Saúde Lia e Sperança* – In 2017 which was approved in 2018 by the government health officials in order to help reduce the mortality rate among children and expectant mothers. The Sisters of *Carmelitas de São José* are the ones running it, and they are doing a good job. As things stand right now, this is the best equipped health facility in the *município* apart from the General Hospital which is located at the Local Government Centre in Muxaluando. People come from near and far in order to be treated or buy medicine. As a matter of fact, sometimes people even come from the General Hospital in order to buy medicine. There is also a system in which some catechists (who are known to be trustworthy) could come and take some tablets to their villages and sell, and then later bring the money.

Apart from this, we also try to give a helping hand to the physically and mentally challenged. We have visitation of the sick every Thursday. We pray with them and those who are communicants receive Communion and sometimes make their Confession on that day. We usually collaborate with the sisters in this area. Apart from this, we also have a group of Friends of the Sick of St. Camillus of Lellis whose apostolate is to also visit the sick, pray with them and assist in doing some cleaning in their houses. We try to help some of them who need the assistance of walking aids such as wheel chairs, crutches, and so on by providing these items. In addition to these, the Sisters also help sometimes with food and medicine when there is an obvious need.

General reflection from the experience

From the personal point of view

Nambuangongo is a very tough mission! The people do not seem to be responding positively to missionary efforts, except for very few. It is difficult to break through their deafness and speak to them about God and the Church. We have tried frequently to visit people in their houses and talk to them about the necessity of religion, but they do not respond. More difficult still is trying to bring back former members to the Church. Some always promise to come "next Sunday", but for months now they have never appeared in the Church. Most of those who come are not ready to leave behind polygamy and other practices and beliefs in order for them to be baptised and receive Holy Communion. Children and youths are not interested in catechism. The catechists tell me the same story in their outstations. Worst of all, we have among the catechists, some who are not communicants and even not baptised. And so in some outstations, there is not even a single communicant and no catechism going on at all.

This is difficult to understand given the fact that Christianity first came to this area (in the 1950s) much earlier than many other places that I know including my own village. This is sometimes discouraging to me as a person. But there are three things that personally help my reflection and give me some sort of consolation. The first is that at least we have a few who are very much committed in the midst of all these challenges. These for me are like the remnants of the people of Israel (Ezr 9: 8; Is 10: 19.21-22; Hg 1: 12). God naturally uses remnants for His work of rebuilding and restoration. So I often ask myself: could these faithful and generous people be the remnants of Nambuangongo through whom God will rebuild and heal the land?

Another thing that helps my reflection and gives me some sort of consolation is the fact that while I do not seem to be achieving much in my missionary endeavours, at least I am learning some lessons about patience and humility. There were times I was so impatient that I began to say to myself: "Could it be that I do not have the missionary qualities to work in this place?" But I am beginning to discover that sometimes these qualities are learnt rather than inherent. The few months I have stayed here have taught me the real meaning of sacrifice. I have learned that priesthood is not only about celebrating Mass and the other sacraments and attending to people in the office. It also means going out to meet people on the streets and in their houses, and sometimes even on their farms in order to speak to them about Christ and the Church. Perhaps the virtues I am now learning will one day become powerful tools for evangelisation. Patience is needed because we need to understand the people and to accompany them in whatever situation they find themselves. Humility is needed because it helps me to accept that I cannot do it all alone. Therefore I need the help and support of others.

For the mission of the Church

The church needs to prioritize evangelisation. It appears that we are very comfortable with creating and maintaining parishes and various groups and societies in towns and other areas where the Church is already in existence. The Church needs to invest more in rural evangelisation both in terms of personnel and material resources. There is a great need for more priests and religious and catechists in Nambuangongo. Mission stations need to be established at many different locations so that the missionaries can be close to the people. This also means a lot of investment in material resources. Transportation and communication especially will cost a lot given that most of our roads are in bad condition. The Church also has to invest in the formation of catechists and the education of the people wherever it exists. People need to have at least a reasonable level of literacy so that they can read the Bible and some catechism books. In many of our outstations, only the catechist knows how to read and write. Unfortunately, some outstations closed because the catechists could no longer continue to lead either because of sickness or old age.

Furthermore, investment should also cover remuneration for catechists. Our catechists make a lot of sacrifices in order to ensure that the mission advances. Many of them walk long distances in order to come for formation or attend some parish programs. Some catechists even personally cover the normal food and money contributions expected from their communities This is in addition to the collection and tithes that they also give. Yet they receive nothing from the Church as remuneration or appreciation for their efforts. No matter how little, their efforts need to be appreciated in order to encourage them and others as well.

Everyone has a role to play in the missionary work of the Church. We have to salute the courage and total commitment of missionary priests and sisters who have fully dedicated themselves to the missions. Nonetheless we must also recognize and appreciate the inestimable efforts made by loyal, faithful and creative catechists, and all the other lay people who are part of the missionary activities which ensure that the Gospel is preached in spite of all odds. During the last four years, there was no priest residing in Nambuangongo. Priests were only coming from town to celebrate Mass on weekends and then going back to their parishes. During these difficult times, it was the sisters and the Catechists who led the people and with their help, the Catholic Church is still present in the area. In this way therefore, we see clearly the meaning of collaborative ministry in the Church. This means that as clergy, and especially as missionaries, we need to learn to involve the laity in our mission and to respect them for what they are doing.

For the mission of the SMA

At the heart of the founder's vision was the mission to the most abandoned. This means, first and foremost, to go to the people who have never been touched by the Gospel and to those to whom some were reticent to go because of the dangers that presented themselves; the difficulties of communication and of navigation; and secondly, to be very sensitive to orphans, to poor families – notably those that are not able to educate their children – to the sick, to people and families suffering injustice.[3] At the time of our founder, the African continent was perhaps the most abandoned because very few missionaries would have come here on mission. We are talking of the pre-colonial Africa in the mid 1800s when most of the missionary congregations we know today were founded. Then Africa was regarded as the white man's grave because of bad weather conditions, climate, and the prevalence of tsetse fly, mosquitoes and so on, that threatened human life in an environment

---

[3] Cf. D. CARDOT, "Bishop Melchior de Marion Bresillac and the Most Abandoned" in Mgr. De Marion Bresillac (1813 – 1850): A Life for the Missions, 123.

where medical facilities were lacking. It was in the midst of these dangers that our founder chose Africa following discussions with Rome.

For this reason, we seek to identify with the most abandoned. This, for me, first of all means identifying territories that are most abandoned, and even in those territories, giving necessary help and support to the most abandoned. I believe that "To know the will of God, we need an open Bible and an open map" (William Carey). It is no great mystery, therefore, as to why the earlier SMA missionaries showed such interest and enthusiasm in coming to Nambuangongo. This also gives me a sense of fulfilment seeing that through my own little contribution, the work of our founder continues to live.

Conclusion

In this work, I have shared my limited experience of working as a missionary among the Kimbundo people of Angola. While the experience is a difficult one, it is nevertheless a joyful one. As I come to the end of this work, one song keeps coming to my mind: "Great things happen when God meets man". As missionaries God is using us to bring His message to the Kimbundo people. The contribution of the Church seems to be very small, yet its effects are seen everywhere. And so as people of faith, we are confident that at the appropriate time, things will improve and the people will embrace the faith wholeheartedly.

... people with Albinism Tanzania

Janusz Machota SMA with

Soeur Amelia Jakubik CSL,
Soeur Barbara Lydkowska CSL
Katarzyna Jurdziak

"The ghost people"

Katarzyna, a Polish SMA lay missionary currently working at Tanga project in Tanzania, had an albino classmate in the secondary school. However, hardly anybody even noticed that she was a person with albinism and she lived as an ordinary student and an ordinary individual. In many countries the issue of albinism does not pose a social stigma or set those people apart; they are not treated differently. Medicine says that "Albinism is a group of genetic conditions marked by little or none of the pigment melanin in the skin, hair, and/or eyes. People with albinism may have vision problems and white or yellow hair; reddish, violet, blue or brown eyes; and pale skin"[1]. It is true that in most countries there are national Albino Societies, which provide some assistance and support for the people with albinism, but by and large they function in the society just like everyone else.

It is quite different in Africa, where such a person stands conspicuously out in the society because she or he simply looks very

---

[1] https://www.cancer.gov/publications/dictionaries/cancer-terms/def/albinism

different from the rest of the people. What is more the statistics say that in Africa there are many more people with this condition than in any other continent. For example, in Europe and North America one person with albinism is born for every 17, 000 to 20, 000 people, whereas in Tanzania it is one in about 1, 500, making this much more common phenomenon. Although an African albino child faces similar health challenges to her/his counterparts in Europe or America, the Africans are much more affected, especially by the ominous skin cancer, so easy to contract in the strong African sun. Unfortunately, these are neither the only nor the most painful handicaps and hardships which the African albino people have to face. Vision impediments or even skin cancer can be prevented if all the precautions have been taken; they can also be treated if spotted early and if there is prompt and adequate help available. However, there is another big nightmare which haunts them here.

In every society, with some rare exceptions, a newly born child is welcomed with joy and gratitude. An African albino baby, by and large, is received in this world with disappointment, bewilderment and even with an open rejection, especially by the father and the members of the extended family. So, from the very beginning of his or her life, the child experiences stigmatisation which becomes its day to day companion throughout different stages of her/his life. This stigmatisation is carried out by the neighbours, classmates or even by the members of their own families. As if this was not enough, many albino people in Tanzania consider themselves ugly, worse, less important and unwanted people. This leads very often to a very low self esteem, causes different emotional problems and makes them feel second or even third-class people. This twofold stigmatisation results in people with albinism being imprisoned in lonely island isolated from the society at large. They go to schools, attend religious services or (in the case of some) have jobs, but they somehow live in another world. Apart from that there is something more hideous lurking for them. In Tanzania, especially in its North-West part, they are being hunted for their body parts. This horrific practice has its roots in some traditional beliefs: by being so different from others, they are attributed with special magic powers as ghost people. Tanzanians throughout the centuries have believed that parts of the body of an albino person used in certain witchcraft rituals and for making magic potions, will bring someone good health, fortune, good luck etc. Another superstition claims that a sexual intercourse with an albino woman will heal someone from AIDS[2]. At Bujora Sukuma[3] Cultural Centre near Mwanza, the guide said that throughout the centuries, there were no burials of albino people, they simply disappeared. People were just told that they did not die; they were taken by the spirits as they were "ghost people". One could say that these were the old times, the dark ages when those sinister practices were performed by some uneducated and illiterate people. According to a 2009 report by the International Federation of Red Cross and Red Crescent Societies, complete set of body parts from an albino, including "all four limbs, genitals, ears, tongue and nose," can bring in up to $75,000 on the black *market*[4]. Having in mind the average Tanzanian salary, it is important to underline that the ones who have been ordering those parts have not been poor peasants, but rich and probably well educated individuals. That only proves how deeply these traditional believes are rooted in the minds of the people and in the whole society at large.

Kabula lived in a small remote village; she is one of eight children and the only one with albinism. In 2010 bandits broke into her house in the middle of the night, took a piece of timber and with a machete cut off her right arm. She was miraculously saved and after she recovered she was placed in the government run Buhangija Special Centre. The Centre was initially created (as were some other ones) for the blind and deaf children but in those days, it became mostly a shelter for the albino children. In the peak time of 2015, there were about 100 deaf and/or blind and 330 children with albinism. This was an effort made by the Tanzanian government which was overwhelmed by such an escalation of the insecurity situation of the albino population in Tanzania. So in response they created those special centres, which at least provided security, shelter, food and a semblance of primary education. Eventually those places became some kind of ghettos, which isolated these kids even more from the fabric of society. Apart from the government endeavours, there were a few NGOs and international organisations, different Churches and religious groups which got involved in providing assistance to these kids (e.g. "Under the Same Sun" or

[2] In Buhangija Special Centre I met a pregnant Albino girl as a result of rape due to that helief

[3] The biggest ethnic group in Tanzania inhabiting the land around Lake Victoria.

[4] https://www.washingtonpost.com/news/morning-mix/wp/2015/03/13/how-tanzanias-upcoming-election-could-put-albinos-at-risk-for-attack/

"Standing Voice"). However, especially in the case of those special centres, it was extremely difficult to monitor and supervise the aid provided from outside to guarantee that it reached the residents. Much too often a lot of various items sent to assist these kids disappeared quietly. There was even an attempt made by one international organisation to take over the management of Buhangija Centre in order to give a hand to the local authorities and improve the standard of living. This offer was politely but firmly refused and that speaks volumes. The Catholic Church tried to help in different ways as; well. Some parishes were bringing food from time to time. A few religious congregations got directly involved in the running of the schools and institutions catering for the albino children, be it in collaboration with the government or starting their own projects. However, all those endeavours were quite similar to those centres they were still institutions with just better or worse living conditions and management. We have to add that some organisations, congregations, religious groups and schools have been reluctant and very cautious to get involved in this cause.

The new missionary call

As SMA missionaries we have been called to go to the frontiers of the society, to the most marginalised and abandoned. For years the missionaries have been doing that in so many ways, incarnating the Word of God into concrete social contexts and tangibly showing God's love to the people they were serving. This love was manifested not only by being ministers of the sacraments but also by taking care of the sick, sending poor kids to schools or standing up for the rights of the underprivileged. The SMA mission to the cause of the albino people in Tanzania originated from a personal encounter, an experience of a particular situation and people, from hearing a clear call to start a totally new and very demanding mission undertaking. After a few visits to Buhangija Centre and talks to Kabula we wanted to make a small difference at least in the lives of some of these kids. We decided to take full custody of Kabula and she became a part of the SMA Regional community. We found a good boarding secondary school for her in Mwanza. Having in mind the number of albino children in Buhangija Centre, we did not want to stop only with Kabula and soon two more Albino girls joined her. During the school year the girls stayed in the boarding but most of their holidays they spent in the SMA Regional House. However, it was clear that this was not the best place for them to stay and certainly we were not able to accommodate any more children. Throughout that whole time we were continually discerning and seeking to know how to make a difference to a bigger number of kids. What was sure we did not want to replicate another centre, another institution, another ghetto; we wanted to give them a home which many of them had never experienced. This was the beginning of the whole new missionary venture now called Tanga House.

Tanga House

It is a home and not an institution; a home with a family spirit, care and love. It was not accidental that the building was planned to accommodate fourteen and not forty youths, who would be accompanied by at least three permanent guardians and maybe also some temporary volunteers. It is a big African family and not a boarding school or a dormitory. The name "tanga", which in Swahili language means a "sail", itself, indicates the main goal of this place. It aims at equipping those children and youths with good and well directed sails to their lifeboats, so that they can catch a strong wind and sail a very long and successful life journey. In taking newcomers the main criterion is to help especially those in most need, most vulnerable and most abandoned through building on their various talents. Tanga does not want to select the cream of the best academicians in order to boast of the successes by having its members being future degree holders and achieving high positions. We do everything possible to encourage and help our youth to study hard, because for them this is probably the easiest way of getting a better future (due to their skin condition they can not be farmers). However, not everyone is endowed with high academic abilities, and we do believe that God empowers each and everyone with so many talents and gifts as to live out a very fulfilled, happy and successful life. We are just enablers assisting them in getting the right wind into their sails. First of all, we ensure for them full security and safeguarding. Secondly Tanga takes good care of their health, especially in respect to the specific problems connected to albinism. The most dangerous and most prevalent enemy of the albino people in Africa is the skin cancer so easy to contract in this climate. This can be very effectively prevented by the application of the proper lotions, wearing of protective clothes and doing regular skin screening. They also get very professional medical care as regards to their vision impediments. Another handicap connected to their condition is dental care which first of all is done through good prevention, and then methodical visits to the dental clinic. Any other medical assistance is provided when needed. Because most of our residents spent their childhood at those government special centres, and some were left there as young as three or four years old toddlers, Tanga is doing a lot of counselling work around their personal hurt, stigmatisation and emotional needs in order to boost their self esteem so necessary to live a fulfilled and happy life in the way every person would like; to choose their respective life vocation, get a job, and be ready to face and manage different challenges of life.

Tanga aims and actively works towards achieving a deeply rooted social integration, inclusion and a positive social change. Even though all the residents of the house (except the guardians and workers) are albino, it is a hub of integration; there are both girls and boys with a mixture of ethnicity, religious affiliation, (or even football preferences). Tanga is focused on helping the youth and kids with albinism, including through a deep social integration in connection with their peers, families, neighbours and the society at large. It is a place of building of bridges, of reaching out, a place of welcome to all. We have been aiming at making Tanga a hub of various creative activities for the local children from our neighbourhood as well as from other places, where we would like to reach out with our message too. This has been done through tuition programs, games, a small theatre, various competitions, films, presentations, games, social interaction and the time spent together. In a way, even though the residents are albino, it is a house for everyone, a house that will promote and defend every life, from its conception to its natural death.

The outreach

After the biggest wave of the attacks on the albino people (the beginning of the second decade of the XXI c.)[5] the government of Tanzania launched a campaign of protection and increased awareness in the society in order to counteract these horrific practices. However, they did not tackle the root causes of the exclusion, prejudice and violence towards the albino people. In order to protect them the centres were filled with hundreds of kids, there were some spots on the TV and the radio educating the public about this issue, some people with albinism took some public posts and places (e.g. a spokesman for the most popular football club or a job in a ministry department). However, the

---

[5] In 2021 in Tabora Region an Albino infant was killed for the body parts.

real change needs to come from the grass roots; it is a laborious, slow structured work aimed at achieving a change of heart. And this is indeed another main objective of Tanga's activities. To actively and dynamically work towards the full protection, promotion and integration of the albino population in Tanzania by addressing the root causes of their exclusion from the society and the violence done against them, with the goal of bringing about a real change. So far we have conducted around 40 mini workshops in villages and schools. For the year 2022 we have planned 100 meetings. Such an outreach is also an opportunity to find people with albinism in need of some assistance and help. One woman approached us after hearing the history of Kabula and shared her story. She had a seven months old baby when the bandits broke into her house took the child and cut off its both arms. The child quickly bled to death. Still now when she sees an albino child she experiences excruciating pain; she sees her own baby. She has never experienced empathy even from her closest family. Even though it happened more than 10 years ago, so far no one has offered her any support and help. This is another task that Tanga took on board.

Coming together

Our new mission project is an answer to the challenge to reach out to our brothers and sisters who, although living among us, yet might be in another world. What does it feel like to be rejected by your own father and sometimes even by your mother? Living within the family as someone who is different or within a group of a few hundred squeezed into a centre, separated from the outside world by a big wall. During the General Assembly 2013 the SMA once again very strongly embraced the way of dialogue and collaboration. Well, Tanga is the incarnation of that action plan and not only by reaching out to our albino children, but this mission endeavour has connected and embraced so many groups, individuals and options. At the moment we are four missionaries directly involved on the ground. There are two Loreto Sisters, one SMA lay missionary and one SMA priest. We live in one community, work together and form a family with our kids. Tanga was built and has been functional thanks to collaboration and dialogue with various agents. The road of dialogue by nature requires a lot of effort, compromise, listening and understanding. It is easier to be a monolithic entity but is it richer and more life giving? A good example of such an effort of a real challenging dialogue is our collaboration with one foundation which has been substantially contributing to the building of the house and some of our needs. These people are very often far away from the teaching of the Church. But what unites us is the hope of a better future for albino children as no one has a monopoly for doing good. Through this difficult dialogue together we have done something good, we ourselves being firm and very clear on where we stand and never compromising on any of the fundamental values. What is more, who if not us missionaries should build bridges towards those groups in the polarised world of today? We have decided to take that difficult road of the dialogue and reaching out, which very often costs frustration, criticism and sometimes even an open rejection. However, we believe that this is the only way the missionaries can follow, especially in such a project.

Specialised mission

The world is changing very fast, the mission context in Africa is doing the same. In Tanzania the diocesan seminaries are full; the majority of religious congregations are experiencing a boom in vocations as well, so much so that some have to limit the numbers of the candidates because there are not sufficient places or financial resources for their formation.

What is the role of an SMA missionary and indeed any missionary in such a context? Certainly, there are still places where the missionary presence is indispensable. These are the primary evangelisation territories, remote and isolated areas or missions of a very specific nature. We also need some more established parishes for the sake of the future of the Society as well as a missionary presence and dimension within a very "diocesan" milieu. But there are also new signs of the time calling the SMA and other missionary groups to a more specialised mission in the Africa of today. To a mission which the local Church and other congregations will not undertake because of either different priorities, charisms, lack of resources or ... the lack of de Bresillac's missionary "insanity"- when he accepted the mission to the one of the most difficult parts of Africa – the West Coast, and when he stepped down from the ship in Free Town despite the rampaging epidemic of the yellow fever. We need some new missionary "insanity" to ensure that our mission is in accord with our to our charism. ICOF, SHALOM and our TANGA are vivid examples of how to make a new and specific contribution which otherwise no one would do. There have been different attempts to address the cause of the albino people in Tanzania by various organisations as well as by the Church. But Tanga has got a totally new and particular way, not only to welcome our sisters and brothers with albinism into our world but also to ask them to invite us to enter into theirs.

Writings of SMA confreres

ALGERI, R. - CATALANO, A. - MANDONICO, A., *Le ragioni del dialogo*, Messina-Civitanova Marche 2022, pp. 286.

BONEMAISON, M., *Naissance d'une Eglise locale. Le Haut-Dahomey 1931-1964*, Tome I, Roma 2021, pp. 429.

DUJARIER, M., *Frères dans le Christ*, Lyons 2022, pp. 118.

FATCHEOUN, K.R., *Jésus prophète dans l'Epitre aux Hébreux. Etude exégétique d'He 3, 1-6*, Paris 2021, pp. 473.

GUILLAUME, J.M., *Prier 15 jours avec M. de Marion Brésillac*, Bruyères-le-Châtel 2021, pp. 118.

GUILLAUME, J.M., *With Venerable Melchior de Marion Brésillac*, Bruyères-le-Châtel 2021, pp. 123.

HARRINGTON, P., *To prepare his Ways. Tracing the life of Melchior de Marion Brésillac*, Cork 2021, pp. 416.

MACCALLI, P.L., *Catene di libertà. Per due anni rapito nel Sahel*, Verona 2021, pp. 207.

NOWAK, A., *Uduszona mlodosc*, Warszawa 2022, pp. 333.

SEMPLICIO, B., *Soyez saints!*, Genova 2021, pp. 329.

SMA/NDA, *"Avec le Christ, toujours fidèles à l'Afrique"*, Roma 2021, pp. 336.

SOURISSEAU, P., *Charles de Foucauld missionario*, trans. MANDONICO, A., Cantalupa 2022, pp. 168.

SMA resources

Many people wonder where to find various SMA resources. Here we give them all in one place:

Website: www.smainternational.info

Facebook: https://www.facebook.com/smamediacenter

Our Videos on YouTube: www.youtube.com/smaollywood

Our Photo archives: http://joomeo.com/sma.mediacenter

Contact your Unit leadership for username and password to access over 75, 000 photographs.

SMAnetFamily:

- You can find the SMA database including ETAT and Necrology online here. You can also see the list of people who have passed through every SMA address.

- SMAnetFamily hosts official SMA documents that are not available in the public domain like various directories.

- We do online elections through this platform.

- Temporary and Permanent SMA members have received their usernames and passwords to access this cyberspace. Every Unit leadership is responsible to keep up to date the details concerning the Unit. Anyone who needs help can contact the Unit leaders concerned and Unit leaders can contact the Media Centre.

SMA Publications :

Writings of and on our Founder:

In PDF format: All writings of the Founder and a good number of writings on him are available for download from our website.
ebook : All writings of the founder are available in most ebook-stores including amazon, iBooks, Kobo and Smashwords.

Other writings of our confreres: We have published over eighty books through amazon. Go to any amazon website and search for 'SMA Publications' to access our books.

Printed in Great Britain
by Amazon